Letters
from
Viet Nam

Letters

from Viet Nam

Edited by Glenn Munson

Designed by Jacques Chazaud

Published by　Parallax Publishing Co., Inc.

and　Pocket Books, Inc.

Published simultaneously in the United States and Canada by Parallax Publishing Co., Inc., 231 East 51st Street, New York 10022; and Pocket Books, Inc., 630 Fifth Avenue, New York 10020.

Printed in the United States of America

Photo credits: *PIP Photos, Inc.*—cover; *UPI*—pages 2–3, 24, 35, 49 (by Kyoichi Sawada); *Wide World Photos*—pages 7, 8–9, 14–15, 40, 42–43, 56, 63, 70, 78, 92, 96, 103, 114, 127.

Photo research: Susan Moldow

Contents

The letters herein from our fighting men in Vietnam were sent first to the Editors of THIS WEEK Magazine, which published selections in a series of articles. Each serviceman whose letter was published in the magazine received a $25 U.S. Savings Bond. We are grateful to John J. O'Connell, Editor of THIS WEEK, for permission to read the thousands of letters they received and to make our own selection for publication in this book.

Introduction

This soldier is one of the hundreds of thousands of Americans who are fighting in Vietnam. They are the authors of this book, as well as its subject. Their letters present a true picture of what they do, what they think, and how they feel.

Going to War

"*I'll write if I can, but who knows? Somebody has to die.*"

Dear Mother,

. . . . .

As Cynthia told you, we are still on Okinawa and there is no word when or even if we will leave. It disturbs me a bit to spend my tour here, but I suspect this one will last long enough for every one to get their fair share of the action. It is difficult to explain one's feelings in terms of this war. The thing is so important to the United States and to the Vietnamese people. With them it is particularly tragic because they don't really know the meaning of freedom anyway. They have been living with this war now for twenty-five years, and all they really want is to be left alone. Unfortunately, there are those in this world that are not content to leave things alone. It is tragic for these people that their country must be the battleground in this struggle. You must admire them that they will continue to fight for something they understand only imperfectly against something they don't understand any better. And of course the ones who suffer most in both countries are those who understand the least. The women and children who have to watch their husbands, sons, and fathers go off not knowing when or if they will see them again. There is a proportionate share of heroes in any fighting force on both sides, but there is a far larger share of heroes in the ranks of the mothers and wives who must sit home and wait. There is one saving grace, no matter what the cost. The fight is a worthwhile fight, and free life that we have in the United States is a worthwhile goal. Perhaps the only goal worth the price.

We are now going through a period of inspections. They are designed to find out how we made out on the move over here and to see if we are prepared to move to Vietnam. We have a fine bunch of Marines in this outfit, but I guess when the chips are down the Marine Corps is full of fine Marines. They have proven themselves in the past, and they haven't changed except for the better.

Well, Mother, I had better close this before it weighs too much to go by air. Many, many happy returns for your birthday, and don't worry about me. I'm as safe or safer with the Marines as on the highways in the U.S.

Love,

Don

My Dearest Wife & Girls,

I love you, Mary and my little girls, so very much. I feel like standing up and screaming, "The hell with it, I'm going home." I'm in Okinawa, and have been for two days now. It is so cold that I'm about frozen. There is no heat in any of the buildings here, for they claim it never gets cold here. Boy, this Marine Corps is something else.

. . . . .

All the young guys here are in high spirits about all this, but the older ones just lie around and read books. As I look at these young guys, I wonder just how many of them will be heroes, cowards, just the regular Marine in combat, and last but not least, how many will not come back. The closer I get to where I'm going, the more the war seems to be real. There is one Pfc sleeping next to me, and I haven't heard him speak a word. I look at him and wonder what he is thinking about. From the expression on his face, I think I know. I hope he will be one of the lucky ones. Life seems to be more and more important with each passing moment.

. . . . .

A little while ago a report came over the radio that combat pay is going up, and everyone gave a big yell, but all is quiet again except for the card games and the music that is now playing. In the back of the hut a few sergeants are talking about all their good times they had at different places. I guess it is best to occupy yourself, but no matter what I do, I can't seem to do anything but think of the past and wonder what is in the future for me. I just have to come back to y'all. I will come back, that is a promise. Oh, Mary, I love you so much. Please don't wander from me while I'm gone. If I lost you or your love, then I wouldn't want to come back. I need all of you to want all of me. We will have a full, wonderful life together when I get back, and no one will get us apart again.

How are my little girls doing? Keep them up to date on their daddy and how much I love and miss them. Tell them we will all be together real soon and daddy won't ever leave them again.

Always give them a goodnight kiss for me.

Love & Forever,
Daddy

Dear Mary Jo,

First, you *may* consider this letter an interim note. I'm just writing it to keep you posted on the last minute scoop.

We're loading ship in the morning for Vietnam. But the best (?) news is that we're making a tactical landing! That means guns blazing and shells screaming and Marines dying. We mounted .50-caliber machine guns on our trucks, and we've got our combat gear ready. The rifle we use is really something. It will fire 750 rounds a minute on automatic and fires semi-auto from a 20-round magazine. It will kill *effectively* at 500 meters! And with a Marine behind it I wouldn't want to be in front of it at 850 meters. Our bayonets are sharp, but I hope to God we don't get that close. We'll be landing in AmTracs just south of Chu Lai and sweeping inland.

So until I get a chance, which may be ten days, I'll secure this. My new address is on the envelope, keep writing and keep the pictures coming.

. . . . . .

I'll write if I can, but who knows? Somebody has to die.

Greg

Home,

After the first day in Vietnam, I can honestly say this beats a gas oven for heat. It got so hot, I had trouble believing it. It was so stifling that any movement just lowered the floodgate of sweat, and you found yourself as wet as if you had walked in a shower.

To resupply this water you'll drink four or five quart-sized canteens a day, or so we did the first day.

I must tell you about leaving our ship and "hitting the beaches." Around 1400 we awoke to do all the waiting that is necessary in something like this. It was a class in human psychology in that every single person veered from his base personality to either hail or show the fear we all felt. Some became quiet and went off by themselves, others were loud and sang in a too-high-pitched voice. Others were on edge and took offense at everything that was said — really, everyone had his own little quirk. I just stood wide-eyed, often with a tear in my eye, clutching a picture of Mom and Dad, and wishing to God I was anywhere but in Vietnam.

After a morning of biting fingernails, we finally walked down the gangplank to our landing craft. We had a thirty-minute ride and as we neared the beach, what do you think we heard? All of us filled up wide-eyed with fear and anticipation, heard band music!

Several days have passed now. You can say to the people you meet, "You know, I have a combat veteran for a son." I have now defended the basic American freedoms by defying the Vietnam heat, mosquitoes, and rain from penetrating one U.S. citizen. Actually, I have done more, but the heat, mosquitoes, and rain seem to be my most prevalent enemies.

I have just received a letter from you. I wish I had a good enough grasp of language to tell you how it made me feel. Although I felt your prayers were with me, the letter spoke the words for you. When I am with you, I just can't act or say how much I care for both of you, but don't ever doubt the fact that there is nothing more precious to my life than my Dad and Mom. I pray that what you have given me in the past, I will be able to use now so that I can be the son that you deserve.

There is nothing to worry about. All in all, I am enjoying what I am doing. There is the excitement, the companionship of friends, and the atmosphere of a unit in the field. Don't feel undue distress. I laugh and joke too much each day to feel right in being the recipient of a lot of anxious moments. You raised a hard-nosed soldier, so don't worry about him.

Give my regards to everyone.

Son,

Jim

The Land

" . . . the surf breaking on the beach . . . the dunes . . . the rice paddies beyond . . . and the Vietcong-infested dark green mountains in the background. . . . "

.   .   .   .   .

I am a Marine, nineteen years of age, stationed in Chu-Lai, Vietnam. When people think of Vietnam they think of war. Let's stop and think of Vietnam in another sense. Through my eyes, Vietnam is a beautiful country.

I have seen her from the air and from the ground.

From the air, she has a beauty that few Americans see. Her mountains and valleys are patched in a hundred shades of green and brown, and between the shades you find an occasional strip of blue, where a river is cutting its way through the land on its journey to the sea.

You see miles and miles of flatlands where the green and brown blend together and produce a beautiful array of color.

On the journey to the hazy blue ocean, you see miles and miles of white sand beaches with dark brown cliffs, which have tear-drops of green on their faces. All reaching out into the sea, with slim finger-shaped peninsulas and smooth crescent bays.

The sky as blue as a woman's eyes and as beautiful as her smile. The clouds with their cotton-like appearance drift slowly across the sky.

From the ground, she looks hard and rugged, but her beauty still remains. Her beautiful flowers that grow in fear of no man, and blossom in the eyes of God, bloom in all colors imaginable.

Vietnam is truly a place of beauty. I wonder how many American servicemen stop and view these things. I wonder how many will write about it. Very few, because Vietnam is a place of war, and in war there is no beauty.

.   .   .   .   .

Dear Jimmi,

The country over here is really beautiful. The day we flew ashore, I marveled at the mountains off in the distance and the rice paddies below us. At the time, I had a feeling of sadness when I thought of the people of this country and how they must feel to have strange fighting men of different countries engaging each other and sometimes the indigenous people, with oftentimes tragic results. It entered my mind how sad they must feel to have the need for such a thing. War is very degrading and, as Voltaire wrote, the "greatest of all evils."

Along with the beauty of this area is the weather. Since we got here the temperature has been very near or over 100 degrees every day. At first I could really feel it, but now I'm starting to get acclimatized, and while I'm aware of the heat, it isn't as painful. To make the heat doubly bad is the humidity, which stays near 95% all the time. I think that this is perhaps the best place in the world to get in, and stay in, shape. One of the big headaches around here has been the dust and sand. I can't convey what it's like, but it is really something to behold. You eat food with dust on it, you sleep in beds with dust, drink water with dust, and breathe it constantly. Today has been the first day we've had any relief from the dust and sand, and I'm afraid we are about to get a taste of the other extreme. Last afternoon it started to rain and hasn't stopped yet. From what I hear, the winter monsoon is just about to start, in which case we'll be living with wet dust — otherwise called mud — for the next four or five months. Oh happy day!

I mentioned earlier about its raining yesterday. After our flight operations secured for the day, I hurried back up to our quarters, which are passable considering all things, and prepared for my evening at the club. Having spent a particularly energetic day, I decided that a shower was in store. I believe that was the most different or unusual one I've ever had. Not the shower itself, but my apparel. Have you ever worn a raincoat to the shower? I may not have been thinking too straight, but it was raining. It struck me a little funny at the time to be wearing a raincoat, combat boots, and skivvy shorts to the shower. I'm happy to report that the rest of the ordeal was successful and very uneventful.

Love,

Dave

Dear Kay:

Since I still have a few minutes of my noon break left, I will try and get a few lines off to you. It is pretty damn hot here, but we have a breeze usually going here in the valley, and the more I sweat the cooler I become when the breeze hits me.

This is really a pretty valley, what with a few banyan and ming trees and the stunted palms along with the small clusters of bamboos. At one time someone or other had a few rice paddies in here, but they are overgrown with grass now, so whoever it was gave up the ghost.

We have numerous mounds that at first I thought were graves, for they are very much like the gravesites in China and Korea. But it turns out that they are ant and termite mounds. I bought a rice-straw mat to put alongside my cot so that I wouldn't have to step on the bare earth in the morning, and last night I heard a hissing under the mat which I thought sure was a snake. We have krait snakes here, and we killed a large green one that was racing around in the trees. Anyway I grabbed a shovel and had my buddy jerk the mat up, and we could see that the ground was covered with thousands of termites. The noise was their jaws, probably all working in unison as they ate the straw mat.

One of my clerks had an experience last night that will probably live with him for a long time to come. He was getting some sleep while his buddy stayed awake on guard, and he woke up about midnight with a snake wrapped around his forehead and face. He struck out and pulled and fought, and finally the snake let loose. It must have been a boa, a small one, for it did not bite him, but the skin on his forehead was broken and swelled up a bit this morning. I never have heard of a boa attacking a man. We had a lot of them in Panama, and some of the natives kept them around to keep the rodent population down. Perhaps it was crawling over his face and when he woke up it curled around his head in self-defense. No matter what happened, I sure as hell wouldn't want to ever wake up that way.

I made a trip to Saigon last Saturday, a distance of about four hundred miles, and came back on Tuesday. It is a typical Oriental city, about three million population, and most of the population is going somewhere every minute of the day. What with trucks, buses, taxicabs, motorcycles, bicycles, pedicabs, pony carts, and wandering buffalo intermingled with the mass of people, it is taking your life in your hands to cross the street. We went there on business and didn't get a chance to act like tourists. The French influence is plainly seen, that part of the French customs that the Oriental takes to. It was so beastly hot there that I was glad to get back to the country. At least we have our breeze here, and at night I have to get under a blanket to keep comfortable. My only complaint is that I can't sleep when it gets quiet here, and the last couple of days we have had no nightly visitors. I don't mind it when I hear the rifles and the machine guns going on the perimeter, but when it grows quiet I wonder if even our people are out there.

I really don't know why the V.C. want to take the red path to wherever they want to go. This is a rich land with lots of sun and rain and lots of untilled soil. They are practically the only country in the Orient that can export foodstuffs over and above what they use, and they have room to grow more. With money from Uncle Sam to help develop the land, they could be the richest country in Asia.

Well, Sis, time to get this over with. Give my regards to Steve and my love to Gayl and the children. Take good care of yourself, and keep bundled up this winter. Don't lose your temper too much with the kiddies. Write when you can, and I will do the same — 'bye for now.

> All my love,
> *Bob*

The Central Highlands

Dear Mother,

. . . . .

The Montagnards are much like our American Indians. They have their own villages, raise livestock and horses. They cultivate the land. Their villages are neat and orderly, and the dirt streets are lined with trees. The villages are laid out with straight streets running at right angles to one another. Our city planners could take a lesson from them. They walk to town with their goods in bamboo baskets strapped to their backs. The men wear loin cloths and shirts. The women wear skirts and blouses that may or may not be buttoned. They are black like our Negroes, but do not have Negro features. They have no use for the Vietnamese government.

We G.I.s go to town on a military bus that runs every other hour to Pleiku. If one is impatient, he can walk out to the highway and hitchhike. Or, if one can speak Vietnamese, he can ride a Lambretta bus for 20 piasters. But if he doesn't speak the language he had best hitchhike. The bus drivers will try to charge 100 piasters. I know one boy who was railroaded for 500 piasters.

. . . . .

Jack

Dear Annette,

Hi, honey. How are you today?

About twenty miles to my left is the Cambodian border. We will probably follow if the V.C. retreat across the border. Directly in front of me is a large mountain where some kind of airplane crashed. All you can see is the tail protruding out of the mountain. To my front is a valley where the V.C. killed 5,000 Frenchmen. The graves look like hundreds of dots on the mountainside.

The scenery around here is beautiful. Everything is green except this large clearing that we're camped on. All we have is red dust and termites. Last night I heard a funny noise, like sand rolling down the roof of the tent. I got a flashlight and checked. There was nothing, but the noise kept getting louder. There are all kinds of black scorpions out here. I finally decided to check under the piece of canvas I used as a floor. And what I saw made me sick. There were thousands of termites under there. They looked like maggots. There wasn't much I could do but lay the canvas back down and go to sleep. They don't bother you if you don't bother them. They'll probably be back again tonight.

. . . . .

Well, I've got some things to do, so I'll close for now.

Love,
Chuck

P.S. I love you.

Dear Mother and Mom,

I wish I could take time just now to tell you all the things that're going on...just can't keep up and pass them on to you fast enough. We've made one major landing and two lesser ones since the 28th. If it weren't for the fact that boys are getting killed over here, it'd be beautiful. The beaches are yellow and wide. The hills are green with protruding boulders. Thatched-roofed (and walled) huts are grouped here and there...black-pajama-clad fishermen go here and there...and our big Navy guns go all day and all night hitting deep into the interior where other Marines have been helo-lifted.

Yesterday I got brave and hopped on a helicopter to take the gunfire ships' gunnery officers over to have a conference with the No. One gunfire man on the beach. He told us that *Barry* had accounted for fifteen known V.C. dead...and that *Topeka* had now chalked up twelve. Of the known 109 V.C. dead now, naval guns have killed 27...now, tell me, does a guy cheer...it seems to bring a sense of pride to the top to know that you're contributing...but how does one cheer another man's death? This's never happened to me before.

The beach was Sahara-like, with dunes and drifts...the Marines were set up with defensive perimeters out to a mile or more...but we sat right down on benches in the middle of some unfortunate farmer's potato patch and held our conference.

We were told that the village just a few thousand yards away had been sending in sporadic sniper fire ever since they arrived ...I didn't relax too much while we were there...kinda makes a guy happy to be in the Navy with a soft bed, a shower, a square meal or two or three, etc., to look forward to heading back to. The scene from the helicopter was striking...half a dozen Navy ships, all turned the same direction due to the wind, swinging at anchor...the surf breaking on the beach...the dunes...the Marine camp and gun emplacements surrounding it...the villages and the coconut (or palm, I guess) trees...the rice paddies beyond... and the Vietcong-infested dark-green mountains in the background.

. . . . . .

Love,

Joe

Dear Shirley,

I'm sorry that I neglected writing you for so long. Actually, no one else, not even my parents, has heard from me for the past several months. I could tell you that my hind end had gotten peppered with buckshot so that I couldn't sit down to write, or that leprosy had taken both my hands and the pen wouldn't·fit between my toes, but sooner or later you'd find out that I've been in good health the whole time. Actually, I've been so healthy that sitting behind a pen has been incentive enough to go stir-crazy.

You'd be absolutely amazed at the picturesque beauty of this country. In all directions, with the exception of east, lush green rolling hills and mountains surround the lowland plain. Majestic white clouds settle down on the mountain tops and seep into the creases between peaks, giving the impression that a large glacier is slowly creeping downward. Wildlife here carries the rich colors common to an equatorial climate. Dragonflies, so long unnoticed because of drab coloring, sport trimmings of bright red, deep turquoise blue, and distinctly mottled green and black. Small fish in a stagnant pond shimmer with irridescent streaks of yellow, pink, and light green. Only pictures can approach reproducing the color here, and even then something is lost in the transformation.

As with all things of beauty, there is a flaw. I don't suppose that war has often been referred to as a flaw, but that's what discolors Danang, South Vietnam. Bombs, napalm, artillery, small arms, and soldiers lay waste and disfigure the countryside. It is truly said that war is hell, for it has taken a near-paradise and clouded its peculiar charm.

. . . . .

Sincerely,
Paul

Dear Mom and Dad:

As we are still having inventory today, I finally have time to write you a letter describing my impressions of this country. Unfortunately, I have, of course, a very biased opinion of how a country should be, and its people. Having seen how Europe has built itself up after World War II plus, of course, our own great country, my opinions are already set. Also my idea of an economy is one centered on industry, not on farming.

To start with, as seen from the air, except for the high land in the center, it is mostly flat delta country of swampy rice paddy and jungle, consisting of creeping vines, swamps, plain old rubber trees, and what have you. What isn't, is dry, sandy soil overgrown with bamboo thickets, which I hate almost as much as sorrel grass. As Charlie, the friendly local Vietcong, loves to hide in it and does a pretty good job, too, you can see why I feel this way. Only trouble is I can, too, and have just about as much patience as he does.

Saigon is like no other city I have ever seen, laid out with no rhyme or reason, with very nice homes thrown in amongst the hovels of the poor. The people for the most part are hard-working — the middle-aged or the older people — but as everywhere some of the teenage kids are a "bunch of punks" aping American styles and wearing hair of extraordinary length. This teenage situation is predominantly in the cities, while those who live and work in the smaller towns and farm communities are as hard-working as their elders. One big problem as far as I can see is the fact that there is extensive hiring of civilian laborers to do the dirty and hard work, which enables the V.C. to get a very good idea of our strength and deployment so that when he comes back at night he knows just where to light with his mortars and such.

. . . . . .

Jim, Jr.

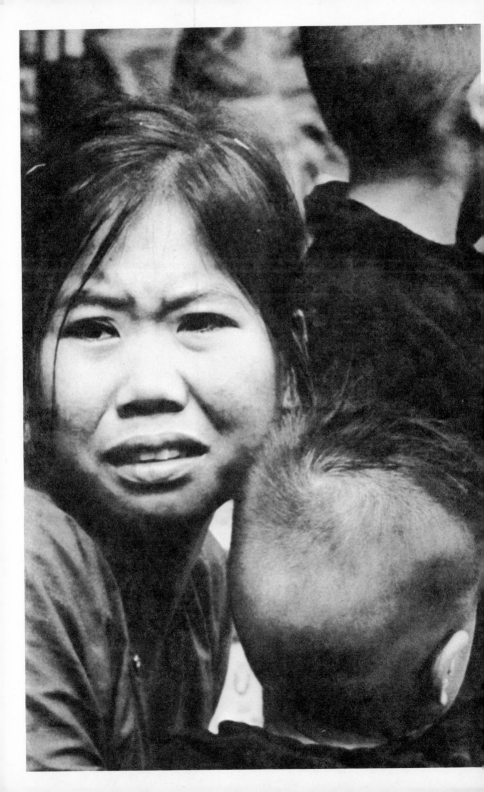

The People

"...friendly and very proud of their heritage, what little they do have."

Dear Melaine,

I don't know exactly how to answer your letter, but I'll do my best. But first, let me say I'm not bitter or down on Vietnam for my being here. I'm a volunteer, so what I tell you, you will have to remember, is seen through the eyes of a Marine, and I'm not really qualified to judge this country or its people.

First I'll describe the country, because often the fate of people is more closely tied to the land than to anything else. Basically the land is divided into the delta type and the mountains. The delta is farmed for rice, the staple food of all Asians. In the mountains very little or nothing is grown. Along the coast the people fish, and this provides the other staple food. The people, and by people I mean the humble masses, are born into pain and poverty. TB runs rampant among the old and young alike. Ulcer-type sores are as commonplace as pimples on American kids; this comes mostly from the fact that the people have little or no concept of cleanliness. They, for the most part, have never heard of soap or medicine. The children are infected with worms because of not washing their food. Most adults chew an herb nut called betel to kill the pain of decaying teeth. The young girls comb fleas from their hair, never thinking to rid themselves of them. Venereal diseases of every description infest over half the people. They live on the ground and drink from the fields, which also serve as sewers. The average intelligence seems to run around the fourth grade; few read or write.

Yet these people have a profound love for their families, and especially the children. They can be and often are industrious. They are crafty at making do with little or nothing. And more often than not, the young boy you treat for a sore in the village by day is the V.C. you kill at night trying to blow up an aircraft, so they owe little or no allegiance to anyone save surviving.

I guess this may sound a little brutal. But that's the way life is for these people. I don't think the people or the country are beautiful. I wish whoever said it was could walk with me through the village someday and tell me it's beautiful.

. . . . . .

You've asked how long I've been in the Marines. Well, I've been in twelve years. I've been to Cuba, Mexico, the Philippines, Japan, Okinawa, and the Virgin Islands, and now here. And if I ever get to the dear old U.S. again, I'll do my best to never leave again.

. . . . .

Sincerely,
Sgt. A. L. Dean

Hi Folks,

. . . . .

As long as I am writing this letter I may as well let you know a bit about the customs and living standards of the Vietnamese. First of all, the living standard over here is very low. Although not as low as in Korea, it would be nevertheless low on the list compared to the other Far Eastern countries.

Vehicles are chiefly bicycles, motorcycles, scooters, old-model cars and cycliles (a one-passenger taxi made of a closed-in seat and a bicycle frame, the seat forward for the driver). You can hire a cyclile for about three hundred piasters a day (about $2.80). You can also rent bicycles and scooters for a reasonable fee.

. . . . .

You often see women working on road building, heavy construction and difficult farm work. They are often deft in their abilities with a needle and thread and able to turn out colorful clothes in silks and synthetic fabrics.

The men are all drafted as soon as they reach the draft age of sixteen. Because of their indifferent feelings about this war of theirs, there are a considerable number of draft dodgers and deserters. Of course, this indifference is not widespread, but it does make a substantial enough number to make the headlines in the *Saigon Post* daily. Another major problem are the coups that spring up periodically. These coups are anti-American and anti-war for the most part, and usually cause more violence than they stop.

The children, having had nothing for so long, have turned to begging now that we have arrived here. Although for the large part lovable, they tend to get underfoot and in the way. I think that the nicest group of them that I have met have been the orphans. These are the victims of war, but to see them you would never be able to realize it. They are some of the happiest kids I've ever seen, and the Sisters teach them that we are great people. We donate to the orphanage in contributions of food and money, and I have yet to be unthanked by Brother Rodriguez. . . .

The figures and faces of these people are typically of an Oriental background, but you can note a difference by haircuts. The Vietnamese girl keeps her hair shoulder-length or longer; it is jet black and has a silky, shiny appearance.

A habit over here that they have is chewing betel nuts. They turn the lips red and the teeth black. I am happy to see this habit being broken by the younger generation. The music is also becoming Americanized, and instead of the slow Oriental squealing, they are transforming into a fast-stepping group.

. . . . .

Love
Your son, *Joel*

Dear Laura,

. . . . .

If you could see how the kids dress over here, I know you'd never cry about something because you don't like it, or it's the wrong color. You know, they wear whatever they can steal, or borrow, or beg. Kids begging for candy and food. The girls, most of them, wear P.J.s because they can't afford good clothes. And they only go as far as the fifth grade; then they go to work and work all day.

There is a young girl in town called Lan. She just turned eighteen, and she calls me B.J. I bring her soap and candy and stuff like that, and she thinks the world of me because finally someone has treated her like a young girl should be treated.

. The country over here is hot and muddy right now. It's always raining. The people eat pine bugs, crushed crabs, fishheads, and all kinds of stuff made out of rice and rice jello..... If you don't eat what they offer you and if you take it and make faces, like you sometimes do, they feel hurt and get mad.

. . . . .

Love always,
Brian

To each of the students in Miss Holloway's Class,

I want to thank you for the cards that you sent. To you back in Alabama it might not seem like too much to send or receive Christmas cards, but here, where we are not with our families or friends, it is something special to get personally-made Christmas cards. Your cards arrived on Christmas day and have been read by many men many times, and each man appreciated them as much as I.

. . . . . .

One thing that I have been happy about in being over here is the chance to see how the Vietnamese people live. This area around Ky Ha is very poor, and most of the people make their living by growing rice in the tens of thousands of rice paddies that are here.

Children, who back in the States might be given nothing harder to do than go to kindergarten or first grade, are required here to watch after a flock of ducks that are allowed to go into some of the paddies — but not the ones that have almost ripe rice. The Vietnamese who are your age would be taking care of younger brothers and sisters while their parents work in the rice paddies (if you are a girl) or be in charge of keeping the water buffalo fed or help with the plowing (if you are a boy); they would be doing this instead of going to school if there were enough schools for them to attend.

Now don't laugh, I know that most of you think that it might be great to burn the school down (providing your teacher wasn't in it). But when you stop to think about how much more you have to enjoy in life than most of the people here, and most of it came from people who were willing to work at learning what and how to make or enjoy some of the luxuries of life, then you will realize that perhaps going to school is not such a bad deal after all.

Thank you again for the cards,

Your Marine friend
Lt. Cederblom

Dear Charlie,

I arrived in Tan Son Nhut airport, Saigon, at 10:30 a.m. on the 5th of February. We came from San Francisco via Honolulu, Wake Island, and Guam on a Pan Am flight. The trip was really interesting, especially the brief stop in Hawaii.

Saigon is definitely the most interesting city I've ever visited, despite the ever-present danger from the V.C., and indeed the town is infested with V.C.! We travel downtown in groups of no more or less than two men for protection. All the hotels are covered by machine guns and M.P.s with shotguns.

. . . . . .

If you're interested in medical missionary work, this place would be ideal. Simple bits of public instruction, for example, washing with hot soapy water, would represent 2,000 years of medical advancement to these Vietnamese. Saigon mostly is a veritable garbage dump with the familiar rats, fleas, and mosquitoes; however, the more financially developed areas of town are like the north side of Indianapolis. Some areas of Saigon are extremely beautiful and have fine restaurants, nightclubs, and bookstores, tailor shops and bars. Other areas reek with abject poverty, and believe me, smell like decay and nauseating putrefaction. One can find anything in this town, from Mozart concerts at the Saigon Conservatory of Music to the bubonic plague and starvation of people living in five-family, one-room flats. It's an experience to behold. The prevalent diseases in this vicinity are typhoid, cholera, malaria, dysentery, and several unidentified types of venereal diseases.

The incidence of plague is increasing, as well. Thank God I have been vaccinated against these killers. The incidence of infection by known or unknown V.D. from intercourse with Vietnamese women is about 100% !! The Army medics advised us that the only way to avoid these diseases was to totally abstain.

. . . . . .

I think I may have painted an ugly picture for you so far about Saigon. This is not entirely so! If a person is aware of the various problems here and conducts himself accordingly, then one may have quite an enjoyable visit in the country. The people are very friendly and very proud of their heritage, what little they do have. Their religious practices are interesting to observe, and the economy is so reasonably low that one may satisfy high tastes with no financial strain. For example, I can buy a tailored suit in three or four fittings, made of exquisite material, for about $35. Tailored shoes, handmade of cordovan or elephant hide, cost about $7. A smoking jacket made of Thai silk would run about $6.50. Also there are three universities in Saigon that would provide any cultural activity that one would desire.

When I get settled down in my job and thoroughly briefed on all aspects of Vietnam, I plan to take a course in Vietnamese and then teach English to the Viet students in the evening. This way I can learn more about the people through closer relationships, as well as pick up some extra money.

.   .   .   .   .

All in all, I'm very satisfied with my assignment to Vietnam, and I think my decision to come here will be very worthwhile — many new things to be exposed to and a myriad of experiences never to be forgotten.

Write me soon, as letters will be appreciated.

Sincerely,
Bob

Dear MM and All,

Had an especially nice day today. Received your 12th letter, and I had a real nice trip up to Marble Mountain.

I got off work this morning, changed, and Joe and I hopped on the cycle and headed toward Marble Mountain.   .   .   .   .   When we arrived at the foot of the mountain we stopped at this old French fort, now occupied by the Marines, to check on the policy of visitors and, especially, to find out if there would be any danger in walking around on the mountain. The Marines shot us full of stories about how we would be captured, held for ransom, etc., after which we walked down to the village and checked with some of the local populace. This proved to be a real sensible move, because we were actually encouraged to climb the mountain and visit the monastery at the top.

The mountain is appropriately named, because it is literally a big chunk of marble sticking up out of the ground. There is a carved stairway (two centuries old) going from the very bottom almost all the way to the top.

We first came upon a pagoda-type affair, and that is where we got our first surprise. Behind the building and inside the mountain is the temple. This particular portion of the mountain is completely hollow inside, with a small hole at the top letting in the sunlight. Inside the temple it is wonderfully cool and quiet, with the only noise being the slight whistle of wind through the chamber. The temple has one big Buddha with one alcove, especially for prayer and contemplation, and various other meaningful statues and altars. Of course, everything is carved out of marble, and the floor is highly polished marble.

After taking pictures and resting, we went on to the very top of the mountain, where a Marine observation post is located. The view from the top is awe-inspiring, especially on a clear day like today.

From the pinnacle you can see east to the China Sea, south down the coast to the V.C. territory, and north to Danang and the Marine concentration; to the west are rice paddies and several villages. I took many pictures to give you all a better idea of the wonderful view from the top.

After a laborious descent we passed through a small cave and came upon a simply beautiful garden. Outlining the garden were medium-high trees with large, aromatic flowers. Bordering the path were beautiful white morning glories. The garden is made up of small patches of cultivated ground with sprouts — of flowers probably — coming up.

We strolled down the morning-glory-lined path and came upon several small buildings that appeared to be a school of some type. The buildings were very well kept and surrounded by a myriad of colored flowers and exotic Oriental-type trees. As we approached the patio, we were greeted by two very friendly monk students who gave us quite a tour throughout the school. Behind the school is the temple, again inside the hollow marble mountain. This temple is unbelievably quiet and peaceful, with the beautiful Buddha and the added wonder of many-colored (natural) walls of marble.

After touring the temple, we were invited for a very refreshing drink of water and some welcome conversation about the school, the V.C., and various other things.

School, being of three years' duration, requires many difficult hours of study and concentration to complete. They study just about everything, but especially their religion (naturally).

In their own words, "The Vietcong wouldn't dare attempt occupation of Marble Mountain." This is due to the religious importance of the area.

The students asked us all about ourselves and how we liked Vietnam, etc.

I took a picture of the students in front of the building, we thanked them for their kindness, and they walked us to the foot of the mountain, via another marble stairway. We passed through the village, stopping at several marble shops and doing some window shopping. On the way back to the fort (where I left the cycle) the people were even more friendly. We weren't approached even once by beggars, and everybody said hello, waved, and smiled at us.

I must say that this has been one of my most enjoyable days in Vietnam, and every minute of the day I wished for you all, to share all the wondrous sights that I enjoyed.

We then went down to China Beach, had a typical Vietnamese lunch, and slept in the sun for a couple of hours. Right now I'm a very relaxed and happy person, although I'm tired; not much sleep today.

I had better close for now. Take care and 'bye.

All my love,
Ben

Dear Bev,

. . . . .

In case you're wondering why I'm writing this letter at midnight, it's because I'm on radio watch now until 4:00 a.m. and there isn't much traffic this time of night. Also the sooner I answer your letter, the sooner I get another one.

The temperature here has dropped to between 85 and 90 because it's been raining quite a bit lately. They say the monsoons have already started. If they have, I hope the rain remains the way it's been, because it's not coming down too hard — yet, that is. It won't end for about 130 days, the Vietnamese people tell us.

No, you didn't get a chance to cook dinner for me. I'm hoping that someday you'll always be cooking for me. But I guess that's a long way off. But when you do cook for me, you better have plenty of cold milk. That's going to be the first thing I buy when I get back to the States. It gets a little sickening drinking water all the time. Especially when it's so hot and the water is warm.

Now I guess it's time to answer your questions and tell you about Vietnam.

There is no doubt in my mind about us defeating the V.C. If the Army was over here instead of us, I think we would lose, because they cannot handle the tactics of the V.C. as Marines know how and can do. I was told by the First Sergeant when I got here that this is the worst war we've ever been in. And he has been in three wars. The main reason for this is the odds they have on us. In guerrilla warfare you need ten of us to one guerrilla to be effective, and we don't even have one for one V.C. But within this area in the past three weeks we have killed approximately 2,500 V.C., and they have killed about 100 Americans. So you can see we are doing a fair job. If you could see how poor and humble these Vietnamese people are, you could see why we are helping them. When I first got here, I didn't think we should be here until I got to see and know the people better. They have nothing at all. They aren't living, they're just existing. Actually, they live like animals. But you start to feel sorry for them after a while and want to try and make a civilized people out of them.

To explain a little about them. It's nothing to see them walking down the road and if they have to go to the bathroom they just stop and go right where they are. Men and women alike. They have never heard of soap, television, napkins, and such as that. The clothes they wear look like pajamas. Their main work is in rice paddies. Right below our hill is a big rice field, and you see them out there with their cows working in the paddies every day.

One day I had to go down to the village as a guard while we fingerprinted the man we bought this land from. To wash his hands he got some water and put it in his mouth and spit it out like a faucet on his hands to wash them so we could get his prints. That's just an example of how they live. Also every day we take our trash and garbage to the dump. When we get to the dump the people are there with pans and scoop up the garbage we throw away. It's enough to make you sick at your stomach to see it. But we feel we can help them to a better life by keeping Communism out of here. They are poor enough, without Communism.

. . . . .

Remember, Bev, I love you. Please believe me. If not now, you will when I get home, God willing. Keep praying for me and write very soon.

With all my love,
Ray

Dear Steven,

Your letter reached Vietnam and was forwarded to our unit. I am the company commander of Company A, and the letter was given to me. I decided it was worth an answer from me. First chance I got, I told myself, I would write back to you.

. . . . .

Maybe I can tell you something about Vietnam and the war.

The Vietnamese are basically a poor people living mostly on the crops they raise. They have been fighting some kind of war since time began. Right now they are very close to peace and democracy. They would love to have peace and be left alone. They are tired of fighting. But the other countries nearby won't leave them alone. They want the rice and rubber that are grown here. So we are here to help the South Vietnamese stay free, as they wish freedom.

We are doing many good things for the people. Fighting is the smallest part of what we are doing. We are teaching them to build roads, buildings, schools, airports, harbors, ships, and many other things. We are also teaching them farming and how to use farm machinery. Also about medicine and caring for the sick. Yes, at times we must fight and bomb the enemy. We try to change the enemy before we fight him. When this fails and he attacks, then we must destroy him and his fighting capability.

We are always on the move, trying to win the people's minds and hearts toward peace. For the most part, we act as much like policemen for the poor farmers as your traffic police. The life of our soldiers is hard and lonely, but they will always do their job to bring peace to this country. No one likes Communism, and we cannot allow it to enslave anyone, not even one Vietnamese farmer.

Right now our unit is building a road from Phuoc Vinh to Ben Cat. The V.C. tried to stop us, and he lost the battle. We will continue to build the road and chase the V.C. out.

Sincerely,
Capt. A. M. Slissear

Dear Mom and Barb,

This evening I received your very welcome letter of the eleventh. Yes, there are phones out here. There must always be communications between units. That is why we are constantly checking lines that are down, either cut by V.C. during the night or blown down by winds and trampled on by water bulls.

Lately the weather has been nothing but rain — for more than a week now, almost constantly. It isn't much fun in a foxhole at night on perimeter watch with the wind and rain going right through you.

. . . . .

On the fifteenth I had liberty and went into Danang. It is very picturesque with its open-air shops crowded together with the usual merchants, beggars, etc. Everyone rides bicycles. I rode in a rickshaw-type vehicle, but instead of running, the driver rode. Something like an ice-cream vendor. Some of the children were selling peanuts; others had baskets of goods such as fruit, bread, etc., along the side of the road.

Some of the people came up to us and with sly looks and hushed voices asked us if we would change our military script (money) into piasters (Vietnam money). This is an illegal practice, since they might sell it for more money to the V.C., who use it to further their own cause.

Later on we had dinner of very tough steak (probably water buffalo), potatoes, and broth. Tonight I get to sleep and I'm glad. It is raining right now, and perimeter guard would be very uncomfortable.

We will be pulling back to Okinawa shortly for a rest and extra training. Then back again. I like it here in Vietnam — I mean the scenery — and I respect the people highly.

See you soon.

Much love,
John

Dear Ruth:

. . . . .

Since I've been here I've found myself wondering whether or not America should be fighting this war for the Vietnamese. The people themselves — at least these here in Danang — don't show any reason to warrant our help. In fact, the way I see it, they are doing the exact opposite of this. They have jacked the prices on *all* the goods they have to sell us about 200%. Anywhere in the Orient a Marine can buy a beer for fifteen cents at the highest. The people here charge sixty cents. A good steak in Japan costs about seventy cents — here it costs as much as four dollars (and the steak isn't even good!). These two things are only examples; they do this with everything we want to buy.

You can't trust the people at all. One minute a man — or woman — might shake your hand, and the next minute he might stab you in the back — literally.

They use our aircraft, guns, men, battle equipment of all sorts, and this is what they give in return.

Don't take what I write as gospel truth, because this is my own opinion, the way I see it to be. I get the same opinion from other Marines I talk to, but we may be dim-minded and completely wrong. But I doubt it.

Then, again, I look at it from the political and moral-obligation aspect of it. While we're physically fighting the Vietcong, we're politically fighting Communism. We're fighting, in particular, Red China and Russia. We've promised to help the Vietnamese win their war against the threat of Communism just as we've made our promise to the entire world to fight Communism. This war here could be compared to the battle of Guadalcanal in the Second World War. A small campaign in a big war. Vietnam is the Guadalcanal of the war against Communism.

Love,

Don

. . . . .

I'll tell you a little about this place. It is hot, and it is cold. The people all have slanted brown eyes, tan skin, and black hair. The roads are poor, railroads run hardly anywhere; the main means of transportation is the bike. Americans are treated like a Negro in Mississippi with a white wife. That's not true all over, however; the Prime Minister of North Vietnam was born here, so the people have a local-boy-makes-good attitude. We get shot at once in a while (no one has been hit in two months, and no one from the compound has ever been killed). The people are always looking for a little extra money and will sell their teenage daughters or dive in front of a jeep and claim damages. Whores in this country are in the high-income bracket since Americans have arrived. . . . . . The basic food is rice, and the meat is fish and water buffalo. Water buffalo is eaten when it is too old to work.

The people are not rich, and money is only made by foreign nationals. The Chinese and the Indians control most of the business. The Vietnamese are people that will earn eight dollars and spend sixteen. They have a lot of low-grade gold, which can be found in their teeth and in small gold charms. They will buy a gold charm before they pay the rent. TB is the big killer here, and rabies is running a close second. The V.C. are the biggest human killer, and they kill more cattle and livestock than the Black Death killed Europeans. I have very little concern for the Vietnam life, but know that if Asian countries are going to survive, the Vietcong will have to be stopped here. They can have Vietnam, if they would leave the rest of the East alone. It would be outstanding if the Cong would go home and stay home, but they have too much support in the hills.

I guess the big problem is that I don't understand these people. We can't talk to them, they have different moral standards, and their outlook on life is different. (I feel that if I can't be an American I don't care to be anything. They feel if they can't be a Vietnamese, so what, they are alive, and that's what counts. They aren't willing to give up anything; they only want to take.) We had an accident today; a bike ran into the back of a truck a G.I. was driving. The Vietnamese walked away from the accident, and two hours later the Q.C. (Vietnam police) were at the compound demanding payment for damage to the bike. The person was on his death bed and needed two dollars to survive. This happens all the time; people are willing to let you run over them, if they can get paid for it.

This should give you a general idea of my views of Vietnam. The best thing I can say for it is it is beautiful. It is so green and grassy. The mountains rise up cleanly from the rice paddies, and the central highlands are vast and rolling. The people have not spoiled them with buildings and factories. . . .

In the Thick of it

"... somehow we got out. I aged about ten years that night."

Dear Elizabeth,

. . . . .

I had quite an interesting watch last night. I had the roving patrol — all four hours. Around 8:30 I saw a small boat coming toward us. I walked toward the back of the ship where another sentry had come. When the boat kept coming we loaded our guns. We asked who it was, and we couldn't understand them, so we told them to go away. They kept coming, so we pointed our rifles and said once more to move away. They then moved out. I sure thought I would have to shoot.

They then told an officer, and all of a sudden the Captain and everyone came out. Here this guy was our pilot for up the Saigon River. He came aboard, and we found out we were going to move out in the. morning.

. . . . .

The river was about 500 feet wide and the land was very low around it, with not much place for Vietcongs to hide. It took us until 11:30 to get to Saigon. It really is a big city, but the people sure look poor. When you visit these other countries, you realize how wonderful you have it back home.

. . . . .

We really did a good job of docking the ship. They have a rotten boat dock, and we came in a little fast, right into a chunk of cement. They say cement doesn't move very easy, but you should have seen it fly, but then again it split the seam of our ship. They are working on it now.

We got more different orders today. We load up here, which should take three days, and take the stuff back to Da Nang and then go on our first orders again up the river to this other place. We were supposed to be done with this mission February 20th or around there. If we keep getting other loads to haul, we won't be back to Subic Bay until February 26th.

. . . . .

It sure makes me hungry whenever you write you got a pizza. You don't know how good it makes me feel to hear from you. Well, it's 7:00. I have 45 minutes before going on watch. I'll go on my watch in a little while wondering what you are doing.

Love, *Neal*

Dear Mother and Mom,

Two days ago one of my friends, an officer I met while in school in San Diego in September of '64, came aboard in the green fatigues and beret of a leader of one of the small craft (junk) divisions that patrol the rivers and coastline of South Vietnam...how much he has changed...nine months of never knowing whether the "friendly" Vietnamese he has been advising are V.C. sympathizers or not...never knowing from one second to the next whether the bullets that are an accepted part of every day's activities will get him or not...still the same self-assured, quiet-mannered kind of man you'd want to have beside you in a tight situation, but somehow different...as do many of the fellows now riding us, he spoke seriously but without pausing about the five V.C. who shot at his boat and how he and his crew fired back until the boat and all its occupants were slipping silently below the surface... Movies, TV, books...they prepare you for such conversation...but it's still a funny sensation to listen to the actual story. The guy rooming with me had a bullet go through the helicopter he was flying in yesterday...the messages coming in read like a movie script ...V.C. climbing a tree...two V.C. with rifles running along the beach...200 V.C. streaming out of the hills...changing from green uniforms to black (civilian) "pajamas"...baby wounded...villagers say V.C. came and took all their young men 15 days ago...authorities say V.C. came through two days ago and collected "taxes" and rice...gun positions on the hill...V.C. battalion reported moving east toward beach...one Marine wounded stepping on pungi stick...another dead because the evacuation helicopter sent to get him last night couldn't locate the lights they were flashing to guide him in...On the radio up where I work..."emergency mission... request permission to fire on 803513...receiving small arms and mortar fire...taking casualties...request permission to fire...can you send aircraft"...on and on it goes...

I have to go on watch at midnight tonight...midnight until six tomorrow morning...last night we shot 160 rounds of naval gunfire (160 projectiles) at the V.C....but surely not all of the dead and injured will be V.C....there'll be civilians...and animals... and homes...and gardens...and rice paddies...the whole thing is more than unpleasant...

Twelve on, twelve off, 'round the clock, on and on. I sometimes wonder if it wouldn't be better to have no worries greater than the paperboy hitting my front-door screen with his paper each morning...but we'll be home soon and another side of my life will resume...I'll just be Joe-san and Daddy and "Unca Joe" and "Joe Bob" and enjoy TV...and fresh milk...and green grass... and jonquils...and birds singing...and all those little things that never enter one's mind to love and appreciate. Write soon.

Love, *Joe*

Dear Family,

Hello once again. I realize that it has been a little while since my last letter, but I have been busy as hell. I went to school at Clarke AFB for eight days and am now on my way to Vietnam. I am on an air evacuation run. We will land and pick up the wounded and carry them back to the hospital at Clarke. This plane will carry 70 stretchers and six medics. I know that I'll get sick when they bring those poor guys out. Some of the ones I've seen are shot up so bad it's a miracle they are still alive.

It's no fun carrying 50 or 60 guys who are laid out on a stretcher moaning and crying and bleeding all over the place. It's a good thing that I am not home now, after all the bad stuff that I've seen over here. If anyone ever started talking about our position in Vietnam, and burning their draft cards, and all these protest marches — I swear I would kill him —

People don't realize what's going on over here. It is horrible, believe me, just plain rotten. These poor Army and Marine troops are living like animals and fighting for their lives every day that they are in the field. Some come back, but some don't. I've carried some of the ones that didn't, and it makes you sick. Every time I carry these bodies in canvas bags and wounded G.I.s I get sick inside. You may think I'm like a baby when I tell you that I have cried when I've carried these guys, but it's no lie, and I'm no baby for doing it. No living person that I know could possibly see the suffering that some of these Americans and Vietnamese are going through and not break up a little bit. You read one side of the story in the paper, but believe me, there is another horrible side that the people in the States don't get.

I hate this flying over here — you really work like a dog, but I know now that I am doing my part, too. It may not mean much to the outcome of the war, but I feel inside that I am giving it all that I can. I never felt that way when I was flying 124s in MATS. Most of the guys over here feel the same way. We all put up with a lot more pressure than you would think you could stand, and you work harder and longer hours than you should, but it gets inside you after a little while and you just do it.

I've been sick as a dog for the past week and have never felt as weak and tired as I do now. I hope that I can shake it off soon, but with the rotten food and long working hours and the damn heat it will be all but impossible, I am afraid. There is so much work to be done that there isn't much time left for relaxation.

Well, tell everyone hello for me. I miss you all very much. I'll write again soon.

Love,
Glenn

Dear Jimmi,

. . . . .

Our landing in Vietnam came off very well. We flew off the ship on 1 September, and the flight was very uneventful but exciting. Exciting in that this was my first experience at flying over enemy-held territory. Although we were high enough to stay out of their range of fire it was still a very interesting first experience just knowing they were down there. Right now we're located in the northern part of South Vietnam in the area where the rest of the Marines are.

The flying we have been doing over here seems to touch on a little bit of everything. I've been on large-scale strikes, medical evacuations — for which I'm standing by now, and as a matter of fact have just returned from picking up a wounded Marine out in the area and taking him to the hospital — resupply missions, logistics flights, and aerial recons. I really find this exciting over here and so far have enjoyed it immensely. I'm sure that by the end of my year in "Outer Mongolia," however, I'll be just about ready to head back to the States. I can't describe the feelings I have about being over here, and rather than waving flags and singing "Yankee Doodle Dandy," let it suffice for me to say that I'm glad I'm here, and that I've waited a long time to come. At the risk of sounding overly "gung ho," I'll say that I am a Marine, and this is what I've been trained for. It doesn't make me mad to hear that someone doesn't want to get into the action here. It would be great if none of us had to come at all; however, no one gave us the choice, and after the money that was spent teaching us our profession, we can't expect that it won't be put to use.

I've found out that there is a real war going on over here. The med-evacs that we fly out to pick up are good evidence. It seems as though there is quite a bit of fighting going on to the south of us presently, and each day we airlift boys to the hospital who have either been wounded or killed. It is sad to be sitting up in the cockpit and seeing some of the wounded they put aboard. Besides carrying Marines, we're also lifting Vietnamese. Just the other day I flew out to a landing zone eight miles south of here and picked up two small boys and took them to the Vietnamese hospital.

Better close for now; I know I've left something out, but I've got some more letters to write.

Dave

Dear Mother,

I'm sorry that I haven't written for so long, but we are kept pretty busy. We are flying on combat missions, and we leave early in the morning and come back late at night. We go into an area and set up an emergency aid station. Most of the people we treat are Vietnamese soldiers and civilians. You can see any kind of wound you want to see, from a bullet wound to a face that has been slashed with a machete. Some of them are days old by the time we can get in to evacuate them, and do they stink! You've probably smelled rotten old blood. It's so bad that you have to leave to throw up a couple of times. We had one woman who had both of her breasts blown off. It was a horrible sight. We've had to perform so many tracheotomies that I can't count them. We haven't had to do any amputations, simply because we don't have a sterile field to operate on. We can hardly do anything except bandage them up and start intravenous infusions, if that's the right word for giving fluids for loss of blood. I think it is. It's not

bad! I'm getting a lot of experience out of it. I don't like to fly unless I have to, because once we got shot down, and once we flew into a storm and got lost and had to make a forced landing in a Vietcong training area. We almost got it that time, but somehow we got out. I aged about ten years that night. We all carry weapons. They come in handy when you least expect it. I'll tell you how bad it is. Last week in one morning we treated 137 wounded and 9 dead in one supposedly small battle. I've got nine months and twenty-one days left over here, and I can't wait to get back to civilization. The people over here are dirty, and all of them constantly have some kind of disease. The towns stink, and you get sick every time you go near them. Like they say, "war is hell." I've had tonsilitis twice since I've been here.

Tell the kids I'll bring them some presents from Vietnam when I come home. Do you need anything? If you do, tell me and I'll see that you get it! Tell the kids and everyone to write. Letters are a great morale builder over here for most people, and I'm one of them. I'm not actually homesick, but I sure miss home and — — —. (Well!)

I'm going to close for now. I'll write more often than I have been. Let me know *all* that's happening back there.

Love,
Your son *Pete*

Dear Love,

How is everything back home? Fine, I hope. Everything is not O.K. over here, as you probably know if you read the papers. It is not as bad as I thought it would be. I am not in the 1st Cavalry. I am in the 501st Aviation Battalion. I am a door gunner on a helicopter. I am strapped in the side door of the chopper (helicopter) with an M-60 machine gun chained in front of me. We then fly at tree-top level and look for the Vietcong. When we spot them, the pilot hovers over them, and then I go to work. I spray the area pretty good, and then we get out of there fast, because a chopper hovering in one spot is a sitting duck for a machine-gun nest. I am getting another $65 a month hazardous-duty pay for it. This is the most exciting thing I have ever done.

I thought jumping was exciting, but this makes it look like child's play.

The people over here are very friendly and willing to help you any way they can. They are just like a bunch of little kids. I always carry some gum or candy with me wherever I go. It really makes them happy to get something like that. Wherever you go, there is always a bunch of little kids following you.

I am hoping to get a camera soon, so I can send you some pictures. The country looks so peaceful. You would never believe there is a war going on over here. Well, I know this is a short letter, but we are getting ready to go out on patrol, so I will close for now. Remember I love you so very much and miss you every minute. So write me soon and often, and I will try to do the same.

With all my love,
Terry

P.S. I love you so very much.

Dear Mom and Dad:

I got transferred to the 101st. I am now a flying gunner and crew chief on a Huey. It is really exciting, and it makes the time go much faster. The only thing I don't like about it is killing innocent women and children, kids about Neal's age. But you learn to shoot fast when shot at, and when it is all over you're thanking God to be alive.

I sure will have a lot of things to tell everyone when I get home — everything over here is so different. But I do think that we are right in being over here — the people are scared stiff of the Vietcongs.

I got my wings sewed on yesterday, and they look pretty nice! This place is starting to get on my mind — the heat, bugs, dirt, etc. — but the time seems to be passing pretty fast, so I guess it really is not all that bad.

DON'T WORRY ABOUT ME —

Love,
Your son *Jack*

P.S. You and Dad are the Greatest.

Dear Dad, Flora and Lynn,

. . . . .

I lost a real good buddy of mine while we were in there. He was with us last time we were overseas. One of our own men shot and killed him. Some of these guys are really trigger-happy.

The first day we went out on a patrol, and two of our men were wounded. One of them was a corpsman (doctor). We've only got two of them per platoon. The snipers that fired at us sure got a surprise. When the helicopter came to pick the two wounded up, we all were on line and opened up on that village. Everyone thinks the V.C. had an ambush waiting for us. Even if they did, I don't think there were many of them. The biggest percentage of them were hiding out in the hills, and after we left they came out of the hills and started trouble. Now we've got to go back in. I'll be so happy to get out of here.

It probably will be a while longer before you hear from me again, so you all take it easy and write me as much as you can.

Goodnight for now and write soon.

Love, *Jim*

P.S.   Give Socs a pat on the head for me.

Dear Mom,

I never realized how boys felt when they left their families and friends, until now. No one has the feeling, the lonely feeling of the boys who lie out in the field, shot and waiting to die. I don't think any of them ever feel pain. They just lie there, and think what their best girl is doing at that moment. Or he goes back in his mind and recalls what he was doing last year. He remembers all the good times, no matter how long ago. Out in the hot sun, he goes back to everything that was cool to him; the swimming hole, a cool drink of water when he first got through with a chore, or sitting in the swing with his girl in the evening. Then, as the end grows near, the memory of the times he went to sleep on his mother's shoulder.

Mom, I think about all this, and wonder if I'm doing the best I can.

Love,
Harry

Dear Marilyn and Lowell,

Hi! How is everything going for the two of you and the kids? Just fine, I hope. Everything is going pretty good for me here at the present time.

Since the last time I wrote, a few new things have been happening. Since the last time, I've turned from a nice quiet guy into a killer. That raid I told you about that they kept canceling came off on the thirtieth, but my platoon didn't go. The next one was on the fifth, and we weren't supposed to go, either. About ten o'clock that morning we got the word to get ready.

We went in by helicopter, and after reaching shore we set up outside a village. My lieutenant after a while asked for eight guys to go on a combat patrol with him, and I of course volunteered to go.

We were supposed to search an area that was cleared earlier, but they weren't sure if any Vietcong were left or not.

While we were walking along, a shot just missed the lieutenant, and everyone hit the deck. Just before it happened, I was looking up into the trees and saw the muzzle flash from the rifle. After we hit the deck, the lieutenant yelled and asked if anyone saw him. I was raising my rifle up towards the tree just then, and I said "yeah" as I pulled the trigger. I have an automatic rifle and fired about 14 or 15 rounds into the tree where I saw the flash, and the Vietcong came falling out.

I always wondered what it would feel like to kill someone, but after it happened I didn't feel any different. It didn't bother me a bit, and I sort of felt good about it. I didn't feel proud because I killed him, but proud that I didn't freeze up when the time came. I figured his next shot might have been at me and I beat him to it.

That was the only thing that happened around me, and the next morning everyone went back to the ships. We had a couple of guys killed and some wounded, but just how many I don't know.

Well, I guess that is about it for now, so I'll close for the time being. Take care of yourself for now and don't work too hard. I'll write again soon.

All my love,
Mike

Dear Betsy,

. . . .

  Well, tell Johnny I finally got in to my first one-two the other day. Two platoons of our company got caught in an ambush and nearly got it pretty bad. But another battalion came up with our brigade and got us out of it. Bullets were thick as rain out there. I got the Purple Heart out there the hard way. I got wounded right in the buttocks, almost in the right part of my hip. Boy! was I ever surprised. I just hit the dirt and started praying. I didn't know what to do. They had us pinned down for about 45 to 60 minutes before I got evacuated to the hospital. I never thought I would get it, either. No one does, I guess. Don't tell Mama and the rest about it, because I haven't written to them about it yet and besides, it would only make them worry more. Take care of yourself and write soon. Remember I always think of you and love you.

With love,
Danny

. . . . .

  I'm okay now, after they took the shrapnel out of my left hand. It doesn't even look like it will leave much of a scar.

  Well, it looks like things get worse over here every day, instead of better.

  I've had 16 people in my squad in the past month, and now we've only got five left. Three got transferred, seven got wounded, four of them bad, and two of them got killed, to make a total of what used to be a 16-man squad.

  That's war, I guess. Everybody says, and I realize now, that war is hell, especially whenever you watch your buddies get killed right in front of your eyes or blown up.

  I've seen so much blood run out of helicopters that pick up our wounded that it looks like the rivers would be red instead of green.

  We are killing the hell out of these Vietcong, though, and I enjoy seeing every one of them fall to the ground.

  Well, I'd better close for now. I've got to lead an ambush patrol tonight, and I've got to get everything arranged.

  Pray for us all. We need all the support we can get.

(The excerpt above is from a letter posted just before the writer, a Marine corporal, was killed.)

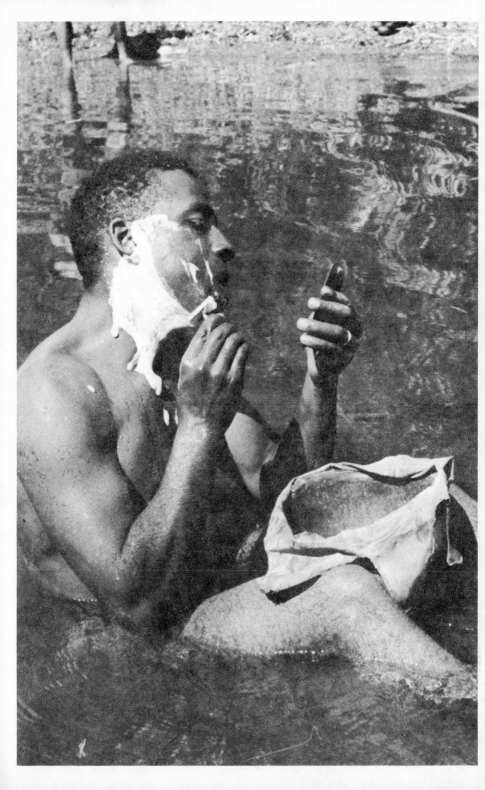

Day to Day

" *... life here is beginning to settle into a routine ...* "

Dear Kay:

. . . .

We have been building a base camp so far and have been fighting off the probes that the Vietcong have been making after dark, but we are going out now to look for the little man. We send a battalion out tomorrow into the hills, and I will take my crew and go out on the fifth. We will be out for something like six weeks, so I am getting all my letter-writing in now. . . . .

While I am at it, I had better give the devil(s) his/their due(s). I cuss the youngsters out in the States, but it seems that when we get them over here where they work 24 hours a day, go without baths for days on end, and eat canned salmon and boned chicken day after day, so far I haven't heard a murmur. I guess they are all lonely and homesick and feel out of place, but you can't tell by the way they act.

This is about the strangest conflict I have ever been in. We live like animals out here in the hills, and the people stationed in the cities live it up like they were at Palm Beach. I will admit it is dangerous in those cities, but the G.I.s wear civilian clothes and go about their business. When we arrived in Saigon we had loaded .45s on our hips, and people were a bit shocked. We had to check our guns while we were there. I felt like a member of a *Gunsmoke* TV script. You can't even drive out of the city without a gun. I met a couple of Seabees at the airport who were drilling a well 20 miles out of Saigon, and they had to wait all day for a helicopter to get them out of there, since it was too dangerous to drive.

We are keeping the aircraft safe from the V.C., but this beats anything I have ever seen. We are taught for years to spread out so we won't present a target, and then we set up here in what is called a bull's-eye camp. . . . . . I know these people use homemade bombs, poorly manufactured rifles, and pungi sticks (sharpened sticks whose points are covered with human waste), which they place in the bottom of deep pits. The pits are covered over and usually placed on well-used trails. It all sounds like something out of Africa and the old Indian Wars, but they did drive out the French with all of their planes, tanks, and big guns. That is the reason I don't like the quiet at night. They are up to something, and I damn well would like to know what is going on.

All my love, *Bob*

Dear Shirley,

. . . . .

After several weeks of constant turmoil, our life here is beginning to settle into a routine. Each morning a certain number of men are required to work on their particular gear in order to maintain 100% operational efficiency. The remainder are set to work stringing barbed wire fences, digging fighting holes and artillery shelters, filling sandbags to protect equipment, reinforcing and flooring tents, and an endless number of other mandatory tasks. In the evening one-third of the troops stand guard on perimeter defense, while the others are allowed to go to the compound for a shower and a few cool beers. Saturday nights 20 men from the off-duty section are allowed a few hours of liberty to get some restaurant-cooked food, have a few good drinks, go shopping, or indulge in any of the other pleasures made available by the natives.

Sunday morning is open free time to attend mass or chapel, or to clean rifles, bayonets, and magazines. In the afternoon and evening, another 20 men are allowed liberty, while those remaining at the site maintain gear. Monday begins again six successive 10-hour workdays to aid the "cold" war effort.

Sincerely,
Paul

Dear Chris,

I'm not the bomber pilot who wiped out a company of Vietcong, and I'm not the Special Forces man who was killed when his outpost was overrun. I'm not the Colonel who made the famous quote, and I'm not the sailor who carried his Vietnamese counterparts three miles through snake-infested swamps to safety. I'm not the decorated hero, and I'm seldom thought about or mentioned. I'm an unknown factor, so it seems. I'm support. I know they can't get along without me. I want everyone to know it, too.

What do I do? I unload ships so the heroes can have ammo, food, and clothing. I'm the one who's winning this war. I'm an enlisted man. I work 12 hours a day, seven days a week. I'm 80% of the servicemen in Vietnam. I get sick and take aspirins, and I even try to brush my teeth after meals. I'm doing the job Uncle Sam thinks I'm best qualified for and spent some money training me to do. I'm helping my country to help another country to help itself. I'm the muscle in the arm that took the bull by the horns. I'm support, and don't you forget it!

Aren't you ashamed of yourself? These people need our help to stay free! Honey, what you said almost makes me cry, you care so little.

Joe

Dear Sirs:

Thought I would drop a line to the menfolk of the family. I appreciated the correspondence and the news clippings. I can't believe that about O.S.U. and Oregon beating U.C.L.A. Keep the info coming.

I returned from a two-day patrol this morning and I've been lying around most of the day after my bath in the rice paddy. Dirty, but refreshing. Big day two days ago. Robert Mitchum flew out to our company command post. He shot the bull with the troops for a while and then left. I got two pictures of him, but I'm afraid his back was turned in one. I'll send the roll when I'm through. Also, I *did not* get the pics in San Francisco, so please send when you receive them.

The worst thing about this war is the politics. We just aren't given a free hand to work. Always have to watch how the people are treated. They all know where the V.C. are, because there are *no* men between the ages of 14 and 50 in the area, but there are hundreds of very young children. However, if you rough up the civilians to get info about hidden weapons and the men, you stand a good chance of being shafted by the Old Man. It's like telling someone to dig a hole in sand with a thimble.

As the sun sets behind Hill 327, throwing a rosy hue upon the "Horseshoe" and the sound of gunfire and artillery floats gently out of the west, I must sign off.

Your son and grandson,
Bill

Dear Aunt Dot,

This tour of duty is my fourth one overseas and this one is for one year. All of my overseas assignments I volunteered for, including for Vietnam. Quite a few people have told me I was nuts to volunteer to come here as it's a senseless, useless war.

I emphatically told them (pardon the expression), "Go to hell." I guess people just don't understand why we American fighting men shed our blood in a country such as Vietnam.

These people have been invaded by not only North Vietnamese troops, but Red Chinese troops as well.

The Communists have every intention of taking all of Southeast Asia, while the democratic people are content to die to keep them out. We talk of peace, but still there is none. I personally believe the North Vietnamese people want peace, but Red China has a hammer over her head.

The allied naval and air forces are breaking the North Vietnamese's back, while the allied ground force are all but annihilating the invading armies. Still, no peace. I wonder how much more punishment the North Vietnamese can endure.

I am 100% against pulling out of Southeast Asia. To do so, in my opinion, is to quit halfway through a job, and I'm not made of that kind of stuff. I think if ex-President Truman had let General MacArthur go into China during the Korean War, we wouldn't be in this mess today. China must be stopped. If not, it will be just a matter of time before China gets brave enough to try an all-out invasion of India, Laos, Cambodia, Thailand, Vietnam, and others, and we'd better expect it.

I'm working in a communications center about seven miles southeast of Saigon in War Zone D. Our compound is near a small village called Phu Lam. Many, many times the Vietcong have tried to overrun our defenses, but we've held fast. There are elements of South Vietnamese Rangers and U. S. forces outlying around our perimeter. Those boys deserve a real hero's thanks. They have stopped the Vietcong numerous times from slipping through. If the V.C. can get close enough to us, they'll no doubt drop mortar rounds into the compound and then run off. The Cong realize they can't get ground troops in and hold it for long. They also know that we are definitely hurting them by our communications.

Everything that happens in Vietnam — past, present, and future — goes through our station. The V.C. know that without our station operation their chances for more victories increase. Without us, many troop movements would be slowed up, and many air strikes canceled.

So we're doing a good job, fighting and communicating. Both are extremely important.

When I'm not maintaining teletype equipment, I'm training my crew on .81-mm mortar, which I'm responsible for. Many of the troops who work with me are in reality boys, just boys filling men's combat boots. They are kids when they come here, but they leave here real men. It doesn't take long to mature here.

I've been moved since I started the letter, to Nha Trang. About 200 miles northeast of Saigon.

During the daylight hours around our camp, you'd never know there is a war going on. All the hustle and bustle typical of any army camp back in the States. But come the night, everything takes on an eerie change. Flares off in the distance keep reminding us that the V.C. is still around. Sporadic gunfire is heard every night. Outside our barbed-wire entanglements, at the rear of our camp, is a small village. We're in tents now, but it's not bad. The weather here is ordered for tent living.

A week ago yesterday, me and another fellow were outside working and a V.C. sniper shot at us. He missed. We were both shook up for a while. Each time I pass this spot, I seem to pick up speed.

Must go now. Aunt Dot, keep your letters coming, and tell the rest of our large family that I do like to hear from all of you.

My love,
Tommy

Dear Mother and Father,

This is certainly a unique experience here in Vietnam. Working like hell and feeling useless, as if I could accomplish so much more if I were just a tourist over here; broadening my mind, at least. Instead I go out with my radar set (which wouldn't pick up an AmTrac in this terrain, let alone a V.C. crawling around in the bush). My radar set breaks down, but I'm not authorized to fix it. I send it up to a higher "echelon of maintenance," and here I

sit up on the mountain again with a .50-caliber machine gun, infrared sniperscope, binoculars, radio homing device (for getting a fix on V.C. transmission), several cases of grenades, illumination flares, a rifle with hundreds of rounds of tracer ammunition, map, compass, telephone and radio, none of which I have used. All I can do is sit up here all day and all night hoping for something to come along I can shoot at to relieve the monotony. At this point if some diabolical Oriental crawled up the side of the mountain to slit my throat I would ask him in for tea.

. . . . .

Love,
Dave

Dear Laura,

My gosh, so much has been happening lately, I don't know where to begin!

A few days before Christmas, Martha Raye was on board to give two shows. My first encounter with a star, so what did I do? I squirted her in the face at the water fountain outside our office!! Seriously, I was trying to be helpful, but I squirted her in the face, instead! I won't forget that incident for quite some time. It looked just like slapstick comedy.

. . . . .

Then the Bob Hope Show came on board, on the twenty-sixth. What a fabulous show! So many great personalities were here. Everyone was on Cloud Nine for three days, with such beautiful girls on board. I got Carroll Baker's autograph, and also Anita Bryant's. Anita is unbelievably cute! Miss U.S.A., Kaye Stevens, and Joey Heatherton were also here. The show will be shown on NBC January nineteenth (parts of it will be shown). I understand it will be in color this year. I don't know if you'll be able to see me out in the audience or not, but I was sitting in the center section, to your right of the camera tower, about two-thirds of the way back.

Guess I'll close for now. It's getting kind of late. Happy New Year. Write as soon as you can.

Your friend, *Tony*

Hi Sis,

. . . . .

Sorry this letter is so late, but lately I've had an extremely busy schedule. My hours are from 5:30, when I go to work — and we really work, too — to 5:30 in the afternoon. By that time, we're really beat. Then we take an ice-cold shower in our outdoor showers with the wind blowing. I don't think there are any hot-water showers anywhere over here. Then we go to chow and take in an outdoor movie, mostly in the rain. Then by that time, if I'm in the mood, I might write a letter or two. But the only trouble is I'm very rarely in the mood. So as a result, I'm about a dozen letters behind schedule.

I went to Nha Trang last week and went on a small drunk in about a dozen bars. At one place, three of us were in the bar about 10 minutes when three Vietnamese officers walked in and started to drink. A short while after that, while we were drinking and making a lot of noise, all of a sudden we heard an extremely loud bang. Naturally from training we instantly hit the floor and took cover, 'cause there was a big attack there only three days before and quite a few guys got killed. Afterwards you could hear a pin drop. By then we had recovered from our shock and found out that the Vietnamese had fired a pistol. There was a Special Forces guy in the bar, and he walked over to the officer and literally slapped the hell out of him and then kicked all three of them out. Things went pretty smooth after that, until our trip back. About two miles out of town, about a hundred Vietnamese soldiers came out of the rubber plantation in full combat gear with half a dozen prisoners with hands tied behind their backs. By that time we were nervous and had bullets in our rifles. A while later, we passed a group of G.I.s wearing bulletproof vests and still later passed a helicopter flying 20 feet above some rice paddies. By that time, we were extremely nervous. We got back safe, though. Yesterday there were 12 V.C. killed about two miles away, and it stirred up a little fuss, but nothing to worry about.

See you soon, I hope.

Love ya,
Teedy

Dear Mom,

Got your letter the other day, but held off writing until now.

I've got a couple of things to tell you. First of all, you wanted to know about some pictures. Well, I bought a new camera last week because I couldn't get film for my Polaroid. It is a 35mm-slide camera. So far I have taken three rolls of film and have sent them to Hawaii to be processed. I hope they all come out good, so as soon as I get them back, I will send them to you.

Second, the Bob Hope Show was here the 29th. It was fantastic. There was Jack Jones, Carol Baker (wow), Miss U.S.A. (wow), Anita Bryan (WOW), Kay Stevens (wow). I really got a kick out of it. Bob Hope is really funny (I got two rolls of film at the show). It lasted two and a half hours and will be televised on the 19th of January on NBC, so you might get a chance to see me. I talked to each of the girls for a little bit (I nearly went out of my mind). They were all very nice (wow). I hope you enjoy the pictures, when you get them. I'm afraid they are mostly of the girls. Sorry, but that's all I was interested in. Ha ha! The third roll I took around here. It has pictures of me and some of the guys, also the area around here.

Well, that's about it for now. Hope you had a Happy New Year.

Love,
Walt

Dear Mom,

This is the first chance I have to answer your letter. How are you doing now? I hope you're fine and feeling good. I am OK, and we are really starting to get busy with our work. Time sure seems to be flying by. We don't get much sleep because there is always something going on. This night (it's now five in the morning) I got to lie down about one in the morning and then I couldn't sleep because it was hot, and I had to be back up at five for my time on watch. So far we have done a lot in this area. We have treated over 3,000 sick people already in this area. We don't have too much medicine, but with what we have we can treat. They have all kinds of diseases that have been growing since the beginning. They have never seen a doctor. A lot could be done with the small children by just washing them with *soap.* If only we had a lot of soap, we could do so much with it. But it would take so much soap, because there are so many children.

Besides that, we are building a new Special Forces camp in this area. It will be a very beautiful camp when we are done. Also we must go out and get rid of the Vietcong. About a week ago we did just that. We have got rid of some (killed). And also our work includes a number of other things, which it is hard to discuss. Recently we have received two V.C. returnees, who gave themselves up for a better life. They told us that they really had a rough life under the Vietcong.

Special Forces do fight, altogether a different war than the regular soldiers. Our mission is completely different from them. We are located far away from everybody and maintain outposts usually along the border of a country where also we could operate if necessary across the border.

I have received the second package from Evelyn and her last letter. The package and mail is really appreciated but I know the cost of mail is expensive. She said it has snowed there in San Antonio. Has it snowed at home any? I sent Evelyn a map, and I included another cut out to give you some idea where I am. The village Ba Chục you will never find on any map because it's not that big, although there are over 4,500 villagers living in it.

So I will close for now, hoping to hear from you all soon. Tell everyone hello from me. God bless you all.

Bye,
Sonny

. . . . .

I also want to thank you for the greeting cards, newspaper clippings and book markers. The one newspaper clipping about the Special Forces is about the same unit I am in, only the detachment involved is stationed down south in the delta.

As you are aware, I got over here in January, and in very short order I was in a combat zone, an area around Kontum. It's located in the central highlands of South Vietnam, and is about forty miles north of Pleiku. It also lies about forty miles from the borders of Laos and Cambodia. The terrain is quite difficult — hills, mountains, and valleys, with jungle covering most of it. It's extremely hot here, with every known variety of bug, just to make sure you're uncomfortable!

We are in a camp in the outskirts of Kontum which, by the way, is a small village of about 8,000 inhabitants. It is the province headquarters, similar to a state capital, and all the military and political apparatus for administrating the local government is situated here. Of course, much of the province territory is still under control of the V.C., and that is what we're doing here. We put Special Forces teams out in the isolated areas and build camps around which the population of the area can live in security. It's darn near like the forts 'that were built when our country was opening up the Western frontiers. We deal directly with the Montagnard people. There are many tribes of these mountain-people, and they all speak a different language. They are very hardy people, and are of distinctly different race than the Vietnamese. They have proved to be good fighters and have been loyal to the U.S. Special Forces. They've had much difficulty in adjusting willingly to the authority of the government. The main reason for this is that the Vietnamese treat them very poorly. Most of the Montagnards have suffered a great deal from this war — both from the Vietcong and from the Vietnamese.

They remind me of the great wave of displaced persons that flooded Western Europe after WW II. It does help to make my job interesting, though, working with these people and helping them to help themselves.

The War by Night

"We were singing away when all of a sudden a bright flash filled the tent..."

Dear Folks,

This is just a short note to let you know I'm all right after our attack last night.

The V.C. hit the base at 12:40 this morning. I was sound asleep, but I woke up instantly when three rounds exploded within a block of the hut. Apparently the V.C. were aiming at our fuel storage area; it's adjacent to our huts, about half a block from mine. They really had the range, but they were slightly off in direction. One round landed on the road that runs by the storage area. Shrapnel killed the Air Policeman who was guarding it. I think he was the only person killed.

I really woke with a start — not so much from the big "whoom!" but the sound of shrapnel hitting the roof. Immediately when I heard that, I knew it was really close.

Only three rounds landed in this area, but over 40 hit the base — none on the flight line, surprisingly.

We all turned the lights off and blacked-out the area. I didn't know exactly what to do, and neither did anyone else, or so it seemed. I got dressed quickly and put my helmet on. Then I opened our locker and got out the carbines and ammo.

Shortly, we were ordered down to the flight line in case the bombers would be launched — they weren't.

It was rather hairy walking down to the line in the dark, because quite a few people were armed by this time, and everyone was pretty nervous by now. You just hoped you didn't meet some trigger-happy G.I.

We all got down to the line and assembled in an empty revetment. After half an hour, we got the all-clear and returned to the huts.

Overhead and to the southeast (where the attack was launched) you could see armed Hueys (helicopters) hunting for the V.C., but they escaped. There were two A-IEs and C-123 flare ships circling overhead, looking for a target and lighting up the area.

After I got back to the hut, we heard some gunfire near the main gate and saw a flare fired into the sky. We watched for a while, but there was no more shooting.

I had a difficult time getting to sleep, as I kept hearing those three rounds going off, in my mind. I finally got to sleep sometime after 2:00.

Because of my sleep being interrupted last night, I was quite sleepy and tired today, so I plan to go to bed right after this letter.

I heard on the radio that some of the mortar rounds were 120 mm — Chinese type. I don't know if our three were 120 mm, but they were really loud!

Well, I'm still safe and sound, but I startle pretty easily from loud noises today.

Don't worry — I'll make it OK!

Love to you all!
Paul

Dear Nancee,

I received your letter yesterday evening, and it was good to hear from you again. I am fine — just a little beat. I had guard duty last night, so I am tired. We had some visitors when I was on guard the other night. About 30 V.C. tried to get into our compound. You see, what we mainly guard are helicopters. Anyway, a few tried to blow up some copters. I saw them about 20 feet from where I was. I fired a few rounds in their direction, so I might have hit one. You see, the next morning they had an investigation of the area in which I saw the V.C., and they found traces of human blood.

When I was getting off the ship, I said a silent prayer for God not to make me try to kill anyone. Because He's the only one who has the right to take a life — after all, He put us here. He can take us when He wants.

But Nancee, it was either him or me.

Sincerely,
Eddie

Dear Lonely Dad,

. . . . .

Now get a load of this one: You remember when I was coming up here from Cam Rahn and the helicopter backfired, well, this one is really for the books. It's funny now, but at the time I thought it was the end of the world.

This kid Rodger has a tape recorder, and we were recording a song I made up for Christmas.

We were singing away when all of a sudden a bright flash filled the tent and we heard a loud "boom" followed by five or six more. What it was, was a helicopter flying over that shot some rockets off by mistake. They were some kind of flare rockets. . . .

Of course we didn't know this until much later. Now picture this: here we are singing and all of a sudden — flash, boom. Between the first boom and the second, I said, "No, they gotta be kidding me." We all looked at each other in about a tenth of a second, then we all took off. I hit the floor and yelled, "Get the lights!" This kid Romulo, who was behind me, said "Joe, you're not going to find any lights on the floor." And all the time the other guys in the lab were running around yelling things like, "We're being hit, get the weapons, put your steel pot on."

At this time I started crawling on my hands and knees toward my weapon and steel pot. All the time swinging my arms wildly so no one would get in my way. Once armed, we all ran out and jumped into a ditch that was completely full of water. It's been raining for six days straight without stopping.

Anyway, here we are in our ditch with only our heads out of water — praying very hard, I might add.

When all of a sudden these guards walk by laughing and saying, "Did you see the helicopter shoot those rockets off?"

Well, after they were way out of sight, we slowly climbed out of our ditch and very sheepishly went back to the lab.

Now, all this time the tape recorder was on. We've played it all back about a hundred times, and we still go crazy with laughter every time.

Just another thrilling war story that will never make the papers. I hope.

Well, Dad, I guess that's about all for now. See you in seven months.

. . . . .

Dear Mom,

Well, another hot day is drawing to a close, thank goodness. It's been quite an eventful week in more ways than one. Most of it happened the last three days. The one thing everybody was dreading happened. We lost one of our NCOs last Friday as he was helping the neighboring townspeople build a schoolhouse. It was a little after 11 in the morning last Friday, and he was taking a break with his co-workers when all of a sudden a V.C. dressed in a khaki uniform was on top of the wall the men were sitting against, and he started shooting with a .45 pistol and got our sergeant four times. He also gave another guy a flesh wound and shot a Vietnamese girl in the foot. I was eating lunch when a guy told us this sergeant was down at A & D and he had been shot four times. As I was cleaning my tray the dust-off helicopter came, and they brought this sergeant out on a stretcher and also put an oxygen tank in the helicopter, plus one of our doctors who went with the sergeant to 93rd Evacuation Hospital. They operated for six hours, and then Friday they had a special formation at seven o'clock to announce he had died. That's when a lot of guys realized what's happening out here. Well, today we had a memorial service for the man, since he is the first man, not really in our company but in our battalion, who has been killed.

. . . . . .

Well, after the memorial services I saw the Dean Jones Show, which was really great.

Your son,
Larry

Darling,

Well, here I am in a stinking, bug-infested jungle. I can't tell you what part I'm in, but it's pretty putrid. I feel a blooming murderer out here killing all these people, but if I ever want to see you again, I'll have to.

Last night while under fire, Skippy got it. Tony went back for him, but didn't make it. We couldn't bury him, so I said a prayer. He was like a brother to all of us. We'll miss him.

Since I've been here, I've learned a lot of songs, mostly about home and friends. It would really break you up. Skippy made up one that was real pretty. But right in the middle he got it, in the back. His wife and kid are going to take it bad. Especially the kid. His daddy won't be home any more.

Don't worry. There are other fishes in the sea, but as long as I've got you, I'll never need anyone else.

It's depressing out here. I guess anyone would be depressed here. I'd give anything to be home with you, and a roaring fireplace. Man! It's scary out tonight. Every time a branch moves, you wonder how long will it be till I get it? Tony's trying to make up another song. But for a kid of seventeen, he's brave. When Skippy got hit, Tony went right for him, but almost got it.

Everybody talks about girls and home, but most of us talk about seeing a tomorrow, because that's one day closer to you and home and college again.

Don't forget, only *eleven* more months and I'll be home, God willing. Don't worry, I'll be home if I have to go by way of hell, which I probably will. Keep a stiff upper lip and keep your grades up and don't fret none. I love ya always and forever.

Todd

P.S. Merry Xmas, Honey
    Don't forget, I love you.

Dear Mary,

I received your letter and was happy to hear from you. I am in the engineers, and I am a squad leader. Most of my work is explosives and demolitions. I've worked on Vietcong booby traps and mines. I have also gone into Vietcong caves and bunkers with explosives and destroyed them. The work I do sounds dangerous, but it's not really that bad. We also put up the one-hundred-man air-conditioned hospital at Chu Lai. Your letter takes me back to a battle I was in. Maybe you heard of it? It was called Operation Starlite. It took place in Van Thong about 10 miles from Chu Lai airstrip. That was when we heard so mucy about the demonstrations and the people back home who were calling us killers and suckers. It had been a hard two days. We had no resupplies of food or water, because the choppers were busy taking out the wounded. I didn't mind that because the wounded come first. Some of my buddies didn't make it back. This is where your letter comes in. We moved up to a hill for the night. It was very dark that night, and as I sat in my foxhole, I was thinking of my buddies. I asked myself, Why did they die? I thought of the demonstrations and asked myself, Was it worth it? *NO.* A machine gun opened up, and it almost scared me to death. When all was quiet again, I started thinking again of our country and our way of life. Of people like you, and kids like the ones you teach, and it answered my question. My buddies did not die in vain, and if I don't make it, I know that it was worth all the hardships and the price of life for the freedom that we have. Let's hope and pray that the kids who sit in your classrooms will never have to know the meaning of war. I will be leaving next month to go home after a long year in hell.

. . . . .

A Different Kind of War

"It's sure a crazy way to fight a war."

"'They got us surrounded, the poor devils.'"

Dear Mom and family,

Received your letter. Was very happy to hear from you that you are all well. I am just fine. Well, Mom, I am writing this letter in some tea bushes in Pleiku, about 100 miles from An Khe. We flew out of An Khe on the ninth about 3:30 in the evening, and we are pulling guard around 3rd Brigade Hqs. We are in a tea plantation, 4,000 acres of tea bushes. They belong to a Frenchman who lives here on the plantation. He pays the V.C. about $10,000 a year not to fight on his land or disturb his tea. He has about 3,000 workers to take care of his tea and pick it for him. He let us use his land, but we have to keep it clean, and we can't dig any holes. Crazy war, isn't it? It is a real pretty place and clean. The bushes are about one yard high and about one yard wide at the top, planted in nice even rows. So you see we don't have anything to worry about, when the owner pays so much money to the V.C. not to fight on or bother his land.

.   .   .   .   .

There isn't really anything to write about. To me this just isn't a war. Maybe it's a lot different for the infantry, but the infantry is right next to us. I am glad it isn't bad at all, but it is bad enough just being over here for so long. It never bothered me before; I didn't care. But that was before I was married, and now there is a big difference.

.   .   .   .   .

> Love,
> Your son,
> *Donald*

Dear Family:

I have been pretty busy since I last wrote. Guess it was about two weeks ago.

Since then we have gone south of Phan Rhang about 20 miles to Song Whoa for four days. There had been plenty of V.C. in that area, but we didn't see many because there had been a security leak and they knew we were coming and had left the area.

We found a lot of stuff, pungi pits, dart-throwers, etc., most of which wouldn't kill, but would injure a person. We had two killed and two wounded on the way down and back. They had ambushes waiting for us.

We came back to Phan Rhang and were there about eight hours before we moved again, this time by LST up the coast to Tuy Hoa, which is about half the way between Qui Nhon and Natrang.

There are plenty of V.C. around here. The second day up here, we were on patrol up in the mountains. We crossed a ridge, and in the valley below we could see two platoons of V.C. running across the rice paddies. We tried to call in artillery, but we couldn't get it because of the Oriental New Year, and we can't fire unless we're fired on first. It's sure a crazy way to fight a war. Right after we spotted the V.C., we searched a hill up on the ridge which was full of caves, and there was all kinds of stuff in them. Some were big enough to hide 40 to 60 men in one cave. Some caves had some cooked rice in them which was still warm, so the V.C. in the valley below were probably the ones that had just left. They usually hit us just once lightly to test us, and after that they don't mess with us, except for an occasional sniper. Right after we got here, we fell into several traps, but the V.C. got the worst of it. One time the 502nd, which is part of the 101st, almost got wiped out, or it looked like they would be, in a place called Happy Valley up by An Khe. They were out of artillery range and couldn't get air support and were pinned down almost 10 hours. Finally, they had no other chance, so they got organized a little and attacked. This confused the V.C., and they came out worse than the 502nd. From this they have a motto, "They got us surrounded, the poor devils." This was about the last time they bothered us here.

The whole 101st have the nickname "The Black Rifles" — this is what a lot of the prisoners say, or call us. This is in regard to the weapons we use, the M-16, which is all black. They fear this weapon for several reasons. It usually kills a person if it hits them in the arm or leg, which is normally a minor wound. The bullet is just a little bigger than a .22-caliber, yet the force it hits with shocks the body so much it will stop the heart. Also this is the only weapon they can't get ammo for. It can shoot more shells per minute than a machine gun. I can't blame the V.C. for fearing it.

We are in a small village now. Most of the people left when we got here, because most of them are pro-Communist in this area. We are in a real nice house for this country. It's like you see in all the war movies, except we haven't found the good-looking girl hiding in it yet.

Most all the villages we go in, the people are happy to see us. The kids all wave and yell "Hello" or "O.K." to us, but here they look at us out of the corner of their eyes and the kids hide. It kinda gives us the creeps. Usually they hang around, and we always give them candy, but here if we do they stomp it in the ground. We are getting a few to take it. It takes time to show them we aren't going to hurt them, and a few are moving back.

Well, that's about it. We have been taking it easy the last couple of days, but we leave on another operation in a couple of days, and if we get as busy as we were for a while, I might not get a chance to write soon, so don't worry if you don't hear from me for a while.

Love,
Harley

Dearest Nina,

First of all I meant to say how sorry I am for not writing to you sooner. I received your Valentine, and it sure gave me real *pep*. Honestly, I feel like a heel not answering your mail, but I've had things in my mind and at the same time I want time to go faster; I only have until June 21st, and then I should be on my way to the big country.

Since I last wrote to you we have been in at least three search-and-destroy operations. Nothing came out of them except a lot of G.I.s wounded and some killed. We got a few prisoners, and I broke my hand on one of them who refused to talk. He talked! Anyway we got quite a few of them (more than G.I.s) and I hope to stay alive so I can get home.

. . . . .

Thanks again
A Soldier in Vietnam,
Albert

Hi, Pookie,

It has been a while since I last sat down long enough to be able to write a letter. For several days yet, I'll have plenty of time to write. I've been in the hospital for three days, and I still have at least two to go. When I get out, I'll be on light duty for a while, so I won't be too busy.

What brought this all on was a little run-in with a V.C. on the morning of the 10th. We were just getting ready to move into a thickly brushed area that was full of trenches and tunnels when Charlie caught us in the open.

One of the rounds caught me through the left leg just above the knee. It just missed the bone. Because it didn't hit anything besides flesh, it was a nice clean wound. I was able to walk right after I got hit. We made it to cover, and as soon as things cooled off, they got all of us that were hurt, out of there.

I don't know where or how I caught a cold, but I sure have a good one. It's been with me for over a week now, and it sure must like me 'cause I can't get rid of it.

We haven't been given much rest in the past several months, and we have had an awful lot of fellows killed and wounded. Even so, the fellows of the 173rd are still determined to clean up on the V.C.s.

The fellows over here have been putting up with a scorching sun during the day and a cool night. They have been wet, they ate only when they had a spare minute, and sleep is something they dream of. Their bed at night is anywhere they drop, whether it is mud, water, or rocks.

As long as the people back home are behind them, they'll set this country and maybe the world free.

You can't believe what these fellows are like. One minute they are talking to a buddy or charging a V.C. position, and the next they're picking him or what's left of him up and loading him into a medical evacuation wagon. They then return to the battle. They aren't cold-blooded. Far from that, they'll never forget that fellow, but for now they have a job to do.

.   .   .   .   .

Love,

Jim

Hello You All,

. . . . .

We took, or rather searched, a V.C. village yesterday, and I also started *earning* my combat pay instead of just drawing it. We got five of the little stinks. My squad was search squad. I threw all my grenades and borrowed about six or seven. If I heard a rat or anything, I threw a grenade in first. I also threw one in every tunnel, and they've got tunnels that run from house to house.

Just outside the village there was a hutch out by itself, and as we were approaching the house, an old man runs out. We searched the house, and I found a cave just in back of it and started to throw a grenade in it — already had the pin pulled — and the old man runs up and gets on his knees in front of me, pointing in the cave. There was a little boy about five years old that I hadn't seen when I first looked in. I guess he was farther back. I walked around with that damn grenade about 15 minutes, with the pin pulled, before I found a hole to throw it in.

Only one guy got hit, and that wasn't bad.

Remember the swamp, where I saw that monster, *ha*? Well, I'm going back there for a few hours at noon. We've got to relieve the squad that's out there. Another battalion is out, and they figure they might run a few V.C. this way. And I've got to carry the damn radio.

I'm going to put a bar of soap in my pocket, 'cause there's a fast-running stream about 20 feet wide in the middle of the swamp, and I'm going to hang that radio on a tree and take a bath and wash my pants, *ha*. No V.C. is going to come that close in the daytime, anyway, or hasn't lately.

I got a new pair of boots and fatigues this morning. Needed the fatigues sorely. They don't last long when you're crawling around in jungles. Still no jungle boots or lightweight fatigues yet. I could have got jungle boots if I had a size smaller foot.

Well, so long for now.

Love,

Jim

8th

Dear folks,

Sorry I haven't written lately, but we've been busy as hell. We got up at 0300 this morning and moved out at 0500. We're up near Ben Cat again in a rubber plantation, and this is one hot place. We have been here about two hours, and I was setting up my tent when we heard the firing getting closer. I moved up toward the F.D.C. tent, where my equipment was, and the next thing I know is dirt flying up in the area. I was standing up putting on my webbing as I went down to one knee. One round landed about 10 feet from me, and everybody went flat. I jumped in a nearby foxhole and looked for something to shoot at, but we couldn't see anything so we didn't fire.

Captain Jake walks out of the hut with his .45 in his hand and a cigar in his mouth. The rounds are coming within five feet of him. He calmly takes his cigar out of his mouth and asks, "Do we have any machine guns with us?" Somebody says, "No," and he says, "I'd hate to have to use them, but they might come in handy."

The fire slackened up a little, and we moved out in a sweeping movement. We moved about 300 meters when everyone seemed to see this V.C. up in a tree all at once, so everybody opened up, and there was one V.C. less. We went back to guard the F.D.C. The cavalry got three more before it was over.

I've had some funny feelings in my life, but nothing like this. It covered about every emotion in the world, I think, and was one hell of an experience.

I've seen some cool men in my life, but Jake takes the prize with no trouble. Nothing else new, but it was a very interesting day.

9th

Dear folks,

Nothing much new here. Me and the guy I sleep with were lying in our tent tonight, when it was raining, and he said, "Now'd be a good time for the V.C. to attack," and I said, "Yeah", rain and dark," and just then 35 rounds or so of machine-gun fire sprayed the area. So we thought we'd go out and get in our hole for a while

I hear we're supposed to be going back in three or four days, but I kind of doubt it; hunting's been pretty good.

We've got some "legs" (non-paratroopers) from the eight-inchers working in here and I've seen some sorry people, but these fat slobs are something else again. Should have seen this fat first lieutenant yesterday. When the shooting started, he drops to his stomach and does the low crawl out of the tent and then lies there with his mouth open groping for air like a fish out of water. He didn't even have enough sense to get his .45 out. Nothing else new, so 'bye for now.

10th

Dear folks,

Nothing new here. We were supposed to go back in today, but they extended us five days, which is all right with me as long as we don't move. This position is the best we've ever been in, as far as I'm concerned. The trees keep it really cool and nice. Nothing else new, so 'bye for now.

13th

Dear folks,

Nothing much new. I went on another patrol today out front of the infantry. We didn't run into any V.C., but we shot a couple of pigs, wrung a couple chickens' necks, burned a house, and took some rice and peanuts. So we did OK and had a lot of fun. It suddenly dawned on me out there, "Are we the good guys or the bad guys?" We went out to map the V.C. trenches and look for ammo, guns, etc.

We're going back to Bien Hoa tomorrow, and I wish we weren't. I figure I should be on KP about the day after tomorrow.

Nothing else new, so 'bye for now.

Dear folks,

Well, I'm back. We only stayed out about nine hours. Just enough to give them a hand picking up lines.

This was undoubtedly our most successful operation, but we paid for it, too. After I wrote my last letter I went over to the hospital and helped unload wounded all morning. Platoons were coming in with three or four men left alive — and those wounded. B Company alone had 43 killed, 89 wounded at noon today. They were bringing in wounded that had been hit yesterday, and they couldn't get them out. They piled the dead up on the landing zone and left them. They couldn't bring them out until they had all the wounded out. They were bringing the dead wrapped in blankets, hanging in cargo nets under the copters.

As of 1800 tonight we've killed 600 V.C. in five days (this is confirmed body count) and I've had reports going as high as 900, but not from reliable sources. The artillery was responsible for over half of all V.C. dead. The V.C. had a reinforced armor unit and used flame throwers, human-wave attacks, and bugle charges, and would line up four men abreast with M-60s and charge a company.

I once said duty here isn't bad. I was wrong. It's HELL. I hope to leave this place and never see it again.

Love,
Mike

Dear Carol and Family,

. . . . .

Operation Mastiff began on 21 February and was to have been the biggest campaign of the war effort. Operation Mastiff terminated 26 February, a complete flop.

The purpose of this problem was to push Charlie from his entrenchments on the Michelin Rubber Plantation. Charlie was to have run through the only exit to the Saigon River, where he would meet heavy artillery fire and the outstretched arms of the 25th Division. The entire program was in the hands of the Big Red

One, with additional help from the 25th Division and units of the Australian artillery battalion.

At 3:30 a.m., 21 February, we received our march order and by 3:45 a.m. were on the road headed for a position in the heart of V.C. territory. Our position was in an area which had seen no government or allied forces in eight years. Because of this our arrival was a complete surprise and marked only by the cold receptions we received as we drove our way through the V.C. hamlets. Written on the people's faces — fear, frustration, helplessness, hate.

For years these people had lived quietly and in relative safety. For years they had been paying for this peace with the rice they could have sold for profit. They were afraid now that because they had permitted the Vietcong to subjugate them, they would suffer under our guns. They hated us, for we would kill their sons as they fought with the V.C. against us. We were not the liberation army.

Our position was in the center of a large field that must have produced peanuts at some time in the past. To the north and west was dense jungle; to the south, some vegetable gardens and some rice paddies. To the east was some wasteland and a few houses immediately evacuated when our arrival became imminent. There was not a native around.

It took us only a few short minutes to get our guns operational and start firing missions called down by the 25th Division infantrymen. In our spare moments during the afternoon we dug foxholes. Lots of foxholes — deep and covered ones. By nightfall a small city had sprung up, complete with telephones and telephone poles (made of bamboo).

We were finishing our supper of C-rations when Charlie first made his presence painfully apparent. The Australian unit had been hit with .81-mm mortars and homemade bombs. Though casualties were light it became no less evident we were on unfriendly land. Throughout the night our perimeter guards fired sporadically in an effort to keep the V.C. from approaching the unit.

For the next four days we fired at known enemy positions and sampans on the river. Without surveillance, however, we could not know what our kill was.

Every morning a small convoy of two armored personnel carriers and one jeep would go to a town about five kilometers distant for ice. Every morning the convoy was hit with mines and recoilless fire. We lost two privates and one sergeant major.

On the morning of the 24th a small group of V.C., about 50 strong, tried to overrun us. But the murderous fire of our outposts repelled them, and a small group of us tracked them on their retreat and accounted for five of them. The outposts had three known kills, so that C Battery had accounted for eight of the 13 V.C. killed during Mastiff.

On the morning of 26 February we broke camp. Mastiff had been a flop. The infantry never did find the V.C. on Michelin's plantation. Where did they go? How did they get out? All this is a problem military strategists will ponder over for a long time.

Charlie knew that when we decided to leave we would have only two roads to choose from. Since we were in his territory, he had no trouble mining every foot of the way. Our scouts watched while he did it. With this job finished, I'm sure the V.C. were sitting back and counting their chickens. Well — we surprised him. We received our march order at 0630 hours on 26 February and by 0700 hours we were in convoy straight across Charlie's rice paddies, through his rubber trees, and through the bamboo stands. We proved to Charlie the versatility of our vehicles and the determination of our spirit. Such was no small feat. Three of our men were seriously injured while attempting to pull a howitzer that had sunk five feet into the mud. But this could be accepted. Just ask the fellows who were hurt, and they'll tell you, "We sure fooled the hell out of them, didn't we?"

We arrived at Highway 1 unmolested and returned to base camp, Phu Lai, with little resistance. As we traveled the better parts of Highways 1 and 13, the villages we passed through greeted us in a much different manner than did those in the Cu Chi and Ben Cat areas. Children ran out to catch our C-rations cans we happily got rid of. Mothers smiled and continued to nurse their young, and old men nodded. There are not many young men in those towns, as opposed to V.C. towns. These young men are members of the town's "popular force" or perhaps regular Vietnamese soldiers fighting against the V.C. The towns have notices at the city gates warning the V.C. to "Keep Out." And they mean it. These towns *don't* live in relative quiet, for they continually are confronted by the V.C., but they do live with peace of mind. Their towns prosper from the rice they sell. They needn't pay for protection. Someday this will be true of all of South Vietnam.

Well, the hard life I may have been living since I arrived will shortly come to an end. Since we returned from the field our task has been to build a modern Philippine-style army camp on the site of our typically temporary combat-style entrenchment. As a matter of fact, we're actually going to have it quite good. A gravity-feed four-man shower, a 300-man messhall (we only have 112 in the Battery), cement floors for all the tents and eventually perhaps, permanent barracks. The engineers are grading roads through the area and figuring out a drainage system to take away the monsoon rains this summer.

All in all, our life here is beginning to look up. All we need are girls and time off to enjoy them. But now I'm dreaming.

Well, I think I'm about written out. Y'all take care and be good.

Sincerely,
Fritz

Dear Mother:

I received your letter quite some time ago. At least it seems that way. I was real glad to hear from you, like always. Sorry I didn't answer sooner, but when I'm on combat operations I never have the chance. Also we don't carry any papers or pen with us. I wrote to Jowell yesterday, and while I've got the chance I'll write you a few lines to tell you that I'm o.k. and getting along all right.

I hope you are all the same.

I'm located in the northern part of South Vietnam. The place is called Phu-Xuan. We landed here about four days ago. I was on the second wave of helicopters. That was about two minutes' difference from the first wave. We received a lot of sniper fire when we landed. We were really lucky. We didn't get one person killed or wounded. I guess we surprised the hell out of them. I was real glad they didn't know we were coming, for it would have been different. I guess we would have lost most of our battalion. There were newspaper men everywhere taking pictures of us. Also TV men too, ABC, NBC, UPI. Everybody was real surprised to know that we did such a good job without losing anybody.

We killed about 500 V.C.s and P.A.V.N. (Regular North Vietnamese troops). Just like us, well-trained. They were bringing them all day long, 20 at a time. Have been bringing them in like that for the past couple of days.

We also got a lot of guns and supplies, more than we have before in any other operation. They're sweeping the valley right now.

Was supposed to go back to base camp yesterday, but we are staying here till the end of the month. So it looks like I won't get my packages till then.

Has been raining a lot. Today is the first day it hasn't rained in some time. I'm glad, for it gives us a little time to dry out.

You asked if I've seen any V.C. More than enough. Also, have I got any? I've caught a few POWs and brought them in. My mortar helped get about 20 of them when they were in the open. Blew four of them six feet in the air. We support the battalion, so we don't go out like infantry. We sit in one spot and fire HELL at them. I don't guess you know what I'm talking about, but I guess Bob can explain it better to you. Tell him I said hello and that I hope he doesn't have to come here where I am located.

I stopped to eat dinner. Not much of a dinner, but it was something to eat, if you call C-rations food.

Just got our mail. One letter from you with the Valentine card and a letter from Grandmother and a letter from Nellie. Sure is good to get some mail. They are getting our mail out to us pretty fast. Only took seven days for your letter to get to me out here in the field. I guess it's not raining now. It's so damn hot I guess I will go down to this river and swim around a little later on. That is about the only good part about being in this location, but there are a hell of a lot of other things bad to make up for this one nice thing.

Tell Bob to drink a lot, for he might get someplace like where I was. Beer and Cokes are harder than hell to get. But being a sergeant it is a little bit easier, if you know the right people.

Well, I will close here for I have a few things to do. So be good, take care, and write when you can. Tell Grandmother that you got a letter from me, also Nellie.

Love, from your son,
David

. . . . . .

Harvest Moon

On December 10th we left the ship in what we thought would be another raid.

After our first six raids, most of the men start to carry more food than arms. You see, in all those other landings, we had not been fired upon, so why should this raid be any different?

My company was the first company to land, and were we in for a surprise. Our first man had no more than jumped from the helicopter when he was shot in the head. A machine gunner behind me was shot in the shoulder.

They landed us in the middle of some rice paddies, so the only thing we could hide behind were the small rice-paddy dikes. They were firing machine guns and different types of high-powered rifles at us. In the midst of all the confusion I managed to find my squad leader and two other men from my squad. We landed with a 12-man squad; the other nine were spread out in the rice paddies somewhere.

When the word came to move out, I was the first to go. There was a man about five feet in back of me. I had run for about 30 feet when the man in back of me yelled to me and said "get down." I had no more jumped down behind a dike when he passed me and got shot in the hip.

The next time we moved out, I got separated from my squad and found out an hour later that my friend Mike had been shot and killed.

Their machine-gun fire wasn't bad enough; mortar rounds began to fall and killed a total of eight men and wounded 25 more.

It was a long day and an even longer night, for it rained all night as we lay in the water, waiting for them to attack.

I will never forget this day. My squad had two men killed and five wounded. The V.C. lost men also — 3,000 is the number they gave us. I wasn't dry at any time in the eight days we were on Harvest Moon.

We are now on land about 50 miles from Danang. They say this is the front lines. We have been here since the 22nd of December.

On the 1st of January I received a battlefield promotion. I am now a lance corporal. . . .

Your loving cousin,
Art

16 Dec 1965

Dear Winnie,

It is late, and I have the watch over our A & S tent. I am at a place about 24 miles south of Danang with 12 other corpsmen and six doctors. We have set up a small clearing hospital in support of the Marines' campaign, "Harvest Moon," in Quant Tim province, "Fook Valley," near Chu Lai, Vietnam. You will probably have heard by now a good bit about it from the news, but from my end it goes something like this.

We were ordered here, a sandy area five miles off the natural beach near "Fook Valley" (one of the heaviest concentrated V.C. areas in North-South Vietnam). We arrived here a week ago yesterday and at once began setting up our tents — five of them — operating, A & S, clearing, fly, and staging. Shortly after, we began receiving casualties from companies 2 — 1 and 2 — 7 Marines. The first day there were light casualties, but that night the rain began again, and the V.C. used the cover to bring in mortars. They pinned down several companies and killed or wounded over 130 men. The second day the weather had not cleared, and the medical evacuation helicopters could not get in to the dead and dying. Finally, on the third day, the sky cleared enough that flights could go in. I was used to help with the medical evacuation, and when the planes got in we found that many of the wounded had lain in the mud-waters of the paddies (some had died there — it was a mess, and we brought in over 90 wounded that day). We also resupplied the Marines with food and ammo. The push was on again, and the V.C. were now beginning to feel the pain of standing and fighting with the Marines — the third and fourth day brought 600 dead V.C. from action of both land and air forces. We of course were still receiving casualties and were kept busy with all sorts of things. In our seventh day we have killed over 900 V.C., and very possibly more bodies are hidden in caves. Our casualties have been high, with 70 dead and 280 wounded or in some way injured.

So as I sit here with only this borrowed paper and pencil, I am tired of what is going on, but know we are doing what we have been sent here to do.

By the way, thanks for the wonderful letter — no, it won't be a Merry Xmas or Happy New Year for many of us here, but maybe next year it will be, and for years to come, for the work we are doing here now.

You asked if I have ever killed a V.C. On several patrols while at Qui Nhon, I fired from distances of 400 and 500 yards or greater at V.C., and then it was difficult to see if I had hit my mark. Only once have I come face to face with V.C. at a distance of 25 to 30 feet. I carry a .45-caliber submachine gun; some call it a "grease" because it looks like one. At this distance it is not impossible to tear a man in two with this type of weapon. The man was dead when I reached him, but in this place the way life is, one gives no quarter and can expect none in return. It's not very pleasant to take a life no matter how much hate you may think you have for another. It returns to my thoughts and dreams too often.

Ohio is in the U.S. and this is where I plan---

At the time I was writing this a V.C. mortar barrage hit and it is now 0800 — there were only two people hit — all is well now, but it is raining. Write soon.

Love,

Peter

Why We Are Here

"You must stand up and show the rest of the world you're not afraid to fight and back up **What is Right.** *"*

"We are going to win, too!"

. . . . .

And to all those misguided American youths, parents, and other grownups who rant and rave every day that the U.S. intervention in Vietnam is senseless...and we'll never win...

The other night the V.C. killed a man in a village about 1,500 yards from where I'm writing, just because he would not give them rice or food. You see, for a guerrilla to exist, he must have the support of the majority of the people in his area. If he doesn't have this, he has no other means than fright or terrorism left to get what he wants.

That is what happened here.

And that's why we're here.

There are those who go to bed at night in their climate-controlled houses and don't have to worry about poisonous snakes crawling in, the rain flowing in or leaking through the door, Communist terrorists coming to the door at night demanding food and money and giving nothing. But these people, the Vietnamese, have a true picture of what Communism is and does. It is terrible, and it can do nothing.

It promises so much that some of the young ambitious ones fall into these fake dreams...and Vietnamese is forced to fight Vietnamese over the same land, but with different ideals. Communism will never work (but some think that it can be beat into people's heads by smooth-talking dealers of the Communist doctrine). *That is why we are here.*

I have seen the bodies of dead insurgents. I cannot hate these dead people because I know they were doing what they thought was right and what would benefit them the most. The dead men were only puppets, pawns ruled by the twisted-minded men in Hanoi, or even Peking and Moscow. All one could do was pity them for the terrible deaths they encountered.

No, let the smart young college students visit — just visit — this country, and live in the filth and muck that we G.I.s are living in, and ask one of us if he minds being here, and he'll answer them, "Hell NO!" And don't be misled by the remarks of some who occasionally get into the papers and complain about how bad it is over here. Because for every one or two G.I.s who are crying they don't understand and why is it them, there are thousands of us who do understand and would have it no other way. If I had my choice of coming or staying, I would come. As long as there is Communism in Vietnam, there will be Americans here, too.

I admit I'll never complain about rain at *home*, 'cause I've seen ten years' worth here. I'll never complain about auto repairs, 'cause I've walked from Baltimore to New York and back quite a few times with my mortar and enough ammo to do some good. I'll never complain about mud or food that was overdone. No, but let me hear of one person, when I get home, who says that the U.S. in Vietnam is senseless, or that we'll never win, and I'll nail him to the wall and literally dissect his whole ideology on Vietnam and the world situation, because I've witnessed Communism at work and seen its gruesome effects on people's lives.

You could say this has been a time of learning and enlightment for me. I hope you understand how I feel. I hope also that you will have a few comments on the ideas I've put forth. I hope this letter has moved you and set you thinking. And I want you to convey to your friends and classmates (and parents, too) some of the ideas I've given you.

.　.　.　.　.

Bill

P.S. Next Friday we're slated for a combat mission. So Thursday night when you're eating dinner, you can figure I'm having breakfast and preparing to start another day of rooting out the evil that is festering in this worthless little country in Southeast Asia. That I'm ready to give my life in the defense of, "worthless" it will never be! Anything, it can be.

. . . . .

It is surprising how little the people in the States know about what is going on over here. It's not that the information isn't available, because it is; it's just that all the news emphasis is on how many U.S. soldiers are being killed. The war here in Vietnam is not really a shooting war. The actual combat portion is small, compared to the total. We are here in a primitive under-developed country with a low percentage of literacy. In simple terms, being in Saigon is like living in an open garbage dump and it's no different than any other town here.

Much more is being accomplished than people realize. The Vietnamese are fighting a war, and we are supporting them. By we I mean all the countries with troops here. The Vietnam government calls the shots. We have many battles — one with bullets and explosives, and one to win the people over to the government of South Vietnam; if we don't do this, the country will collapse as soon as we leave. One is against ignorance. Another is against disease. Also one against the land. There is one doctor for every 28,000 Vietnamese. Very shocking! The average life expectancy of these people is 35 years; there has been a war with someone in this country for that many years, too.

Also we are building this country; the ports, roads, etc. It is really undeveloped.

We're winning here, though, slowly but surely. I always thought we didn't have a front in Vietnam, but we do. Many fronts, in fact. Every village is a front, and that is what takes so many troops. We are spread all over Vietnam and are squeezing the Congs out. This we will do, and in years to come our troops will be replaced by Vietnamese forces. It is a long process but the only plan that worked against this type of aggression.

We are now moving troops into Vietcong areas where we've never had troops before. These people are proud of their independence and are anxious to have a secure nation.

The countries represented here were asked to come, or they wouldn't be here. And any time the Vietnamese want to, they can tell us to leave.

. . . . .

Dearest Mom, Dad & Family,

Just a few lines to let you know what thoughts are on the minds of us all.

We have the tanks all aboard ready to debark on a seven-day journey into the unknown, where every day is like an eternity, where survival is the most important and meaningful thought on your mind.

Each day you thank the Lord for the men who have trained you to live, eat, and think like the hunted animals you are about to become.

Every step you take is into the unknown, and although you have been up the path twenty times that day, there are always new encounters to elude and deceive you.

It is hot, wet, and miserable, with hardly a noise going undetected, for you know the eyes of the enemy are ever upon you, whether they are at work, at play, or the hunter.

Many weeks go by without a hot meal — your C-rations and whatever the good earth yields are your total diet.

The small amounts of rest you receive between watches prepare you for the next encounter whenever and wherever it may come.

The thought ever-present in your mind: Will I return?

In the many wars gone by, people at home looked up to the fighting man, the soldier who fought and died for their freedom.

But in this day and age, there is only hatred for those of us who are fighting and dying for what our fathers and forefathers fought and died for.

I ask you! Is it worth returning to a people and a land which hold no regards for their freedom!? We have forgotten what it means to be an *American*!!!

I love and miss you all very much. Please write soon.

Your son,

Jim

Dear Mom and Dad,

As I am writing this letter many things are puzzling me about the so-called American citizen.

Is it because Vietnam is so far away that more people don't support the war?

I can hardly wait to return to Marilyn and by then my new-born child, but it's getting so it's safer over here than in the U.S. People complain that the Marines are inhuman or sadistic because we kill first and ask questions later. The people in the U.S. don't understand the ways of the V.C.s. Both the good and bad dress the same, and of course they all look alike. The V.C.s go into town and live with the natives and forcibly try to turn them against the U.S. They pay little kids to throw grenades and other explosives at soldiers, and women have been known to stab guys in the back. What can a guy do who's trying to protect his life other than shoot, too, and hope that he is a V.C.?

We get reports like, "Pacifist slugs serviceman's mother" because her son is in Vietnam fighting for a cause — to stop Communism, and we must before it reaches Europe and from there to the U.S. Do they think that this can be controlled over conference tables? Well, if they do, I hope it's based on ignorance and not through education.

There have been two shiploads of troops returning from Vietnam that reached San Diego and found a welcome committee was waiting for them with signs like "Go back, killers" and others of the same nature. There have been two Marines killed landing at the airport of their home town. Are these people crazy, or what? Do they think we like what we have to do? I'm sure if you asked, 99% of us would say "I'd rather be home," but again we know we're here for a reason and can't and won't leave till that reason is taken care of.

Well, folks, guess I will close here; am fine but lonely as hell, and still so long to go. Please take care of Mar. for me, for I do love and miss her so very much, as I do the rest of you.

Love,
Keith

Dear Mary Catherine,

On this, your first Christmas, you can probably sense, in your own little way, an air of warmth and happiness among those who love you and are near and dear to you. And perhaps, in your tiny heart, you may even be vaguely aware that someone who also loves you very much is strangely absent.

You know, being a baby, you are the most precious and delicate possession in the world. You require attention, love and protection from bugs, germs, and a myriad of little evils. All these things your mother gives you every minute of her day and night. You also deserve protection from a bigger and more subtle enemy, not nearly as apparent to you, but just as serious. And this is the reason I am spending my Christmas on the other side of the world, away from you and your mother — so that next year we can all spend Christmas together in an atmosphere of warmth and happiness.

God love you,
Dad

Dear Mom,

. . . . .

Yesterday I witnessed something that would make any American realize why we are in this war. At least it did me. I was on daylight patrol. We were on a hill overlooking a bridge that was out of our sector. I saw a platoon of Vietcong stopping traffic from going over the bridge. They were beating women and children over the head with rifles, clubs, and fists. They even shot one woman and her child. They were taking rice, coconuts, fish, and other assorted foods from these people. The ones that didn't give they either beat or shot. I think you know what I tried to do. I wanted to go down and kill all of those slant-eyed bastards. I started to and it took two men to stop me. These slobs have to be stopped, even if it takes every last believer in a democracy and a free way of life to do it. I know after seeing their brave tactics I'm going to try my best. So please don't knock Johnson's policy in Vietnam. There is a good reason for it. I'm not too sure what it is myself, but I'm beginning to realize, especially after yesterday.

. . . . .

Love, *Bill*

Dear Joanne,

. . . . .

Thanks for the prayers. With all those people saying prayers for us over here I know everything will work out fine for us.

I've heard on the radio lately that there have been quite a few demonstrations against us troops being here in Vietnam. I think most of those guys are afraid of being drafted. In plain English, they're chicken. They should throw all them in jail. They just don't seem to realize the seriousness of the war over here. Boy, when I get back to the States and find any of those clowns parading around, I'll definitely give them a few lessons they won't forget. Enough on that subject.

. . . . .

Sincerely, *Joe*

Dear Mom, Dad, and Jacklyn:

The battalion is moving out very soon, but this letter carries some bad news for my family. I'm not going to Okinawa with them. I volunteered to remain here and move to another battalion. I realize this must hurt a great deal to learn that your only son rejected the safety of Okinawa to stay in Vietnam. It not only hurts but it increases the worry I have already given you. I am truly sorry for you, but for me I just can't leave, not now.

Many of the men with me will be home with their loved ones on Christmas. I'll be right here, probably sitting in some hole singing "Silent Night" to myself. I know families who wish their son were alive whether he may be home or otherwise. You still have me and the worry that comes with me. I can only say I'm sorry.

So until I am satisfied with what I have to do, I will stay here.

Just add an extra prayer and have faith in God's will, for only He knows what the future may hold for me.

Just hold your head up high and be proud. I'm doing this for my country. Little ole me. Just a very small part, but my effort will not be wasted. I've a job to do and a score to settle, and so help me God, I and my country will not come out second best.

I'm a Marine, and my job is here. I'm tired of playing silly little games. For once I know what I want.

Very often I am plagued by the first article in the Code of Conduct. I want to fulfill the trust given to me by the Corps:

"I am a United States Marine prepared to serve in the forces which guard our country and our way of life. I am prepared to serve in its defense, so help me God."

If defending what I believe in causes the ultimate sacrifice, let it be so, I'm ready at any time.

> With all my love,
> Your Marine and Son,
> *Steve Jr.*

Hi Mom, Dad, and all,

I just received your letter. The days are getting longer, so it seems. It won't be too long and I'll be back home again. I'm so anxious to get back home that it isn't even funny. I'm so happy that Dad ordered my car, and I can't wait to see it. Thank you, Dad, I'm so very proud of you and really, Dad, you're the greatest.

It's hard to sleep, eat, or even write any more. This place has definitely played hell with us. It's been a long hard road, Mom and Dad, and I think I've proved myself so far. I know you all have a great confidence in me, and I know I can do any job assigned to me. I've engaged with the Vietcong and Hard Core so many times, I lost track of them. I've got a right to boast a little cause I know I was right in hitting the licks, just like other good Marines have done and are doing and always will. We've put long hours of sweat and blood in this soil, and we will do our best to get these people freedom. Also protect America from Communism.

I only wish I could do something to encourage the boys that are burning their draft cards to stand up and take their responsibilities for their country, family, and friends. You can't defeat Communism by turning your backs or burning your draft cards. Anyone who does it is a disgrace and plain yellow. They haven't got the guts to back up their fathers and forefathers before them. Their lives have gone to waste if the sons today are too afraid to face the facts.

.   .   .   .   .

There, I've said what has been on my mind! I hope this doesn't bore you, but I just had to put it down on paper.

Mom, Dad, and kids, whenever the national anthem is being played, whether over TV, radio, or at a game, *please, please,* stand up. Show your patriotism. After all, I am not fighting for nothing. *Am I?!!*

We've got to have a flag, also; do we have one?

Dad, try in every way, whether little or big, to push a little of the patriotism kick into Bob and Ron! *Please!* Also religion.

GO TO MASS...

Goodbye for now, and God bless you all.

I love you all.

Doug

Dear Carol & Family,

I'm starting this letter while still hot-tempered over the comments of your last letter regarding the political science class's attitude about this "misunderstanding." I might be willing to accept that this is not a war. All wars are partially due to misunderstandings.

. . . . .

It is vogue to protest, to become a pacifist? Sure, it is wise to turn unto him the other cheek at times, but certainly there comes a time when it must be an eye for an eye, a tooth for a tooth.

Today, the freedom you possess at home is at stake. If we as a nation are willing to allow another country to fall to Communism, then we are admitting distrust in our own form of Government, disbelief in its ability to provide for us. If such is the case, we are nominating Communism and electing to lose our opinions.

I am not being idealistic when I write like this. I'm not trying to wave Old Glory. I am being practical. I enjoy my freedom and will continue to do so as long as our nation grows strong. But every small, distant republic that is victimized by Communism brings the enemy closer to our shores — weakens our resistance. Can you accept that being in Vietnam is a mistake? Should we all come home, only to find the fight has followed us home? I would rather stay here and fight while there is still hope and where I can help others while helping myself.

We are saving our own skins!

Carol — this is what all of us are fighting for here! Remember this.

Fritz

Dear Kim,

Thank you so much for the Christmas card and letter. We just returned from an operation near the Cambodian border, so this is the first chance I've had to write.

How is the fifth grade? You write very well. I have two daughters myself, one in the 4th, one in the 3rd. They write me quite often and keep me informed about what's going on at home. I miss them very much, but plan to be home next Christmas.

I'm glad you are interested in what's going on, and I wish more Americans shared your same concern.

We are fighting the Vietcong (Vietnamese Communists) and also regular units from North Vietnam. Those people would like to take the freedom away from the South Vietnamese people, and we are not going to let them.

Kim, I want you always to be proud to be an American and honor our flag wherever it goes. You and my daughters are very, very lucky to live in America. The kids over here have never seen a television set and don't even know what an ice cream cone is. They do want to be free, though, as you and I. That is why we are here. If the enemy wins here he will win other places, too. If that should continue, by the time you are an adult, we would have a real problem on our hands. So let's stop him here, so that wonderful people like you and your friends can have a happy life in the future.

We are going to win, too!

Best wishes,
Tom Fincher

Dear Mr. Powell,

You will probably be surprised to hear from me, but after reading about the demonstrations going on in the States against our policy in Vietnam, I would like to convey these thoughts to the school. Because in the schools it seems to be where it is all beginning.

I am now in Vietnam, as I have been for quite some time. I have been in combat with the Vietcong twice, and it is pure hell. Never knowing if you will be the next to die is kind of hard to take at times. There was a platoon of 56 men ambushed about a month ago; all but four were killed. In another ambush a few days ago, a man had his legs blown off above the knees. He died a few hours later. Death isn't pretty, and it makes a guy mighty sick at times. But still in the end it is a small price to pay for freedom. Seeing and hearing guys die day after day gets quite sickening after a while. Then to pick up a paper, which isn't very often, and read about the things they are doing back in the States makes us wonder for whom we are fighting. That is when we look at it another way. We look at it like this. We are fighting not for them, maybe, but for the greatest country in the world. The United States of America and for what it stands. And no one, be he a draft-card burner or a plain old demonstrator, is going to change the way we feel over here.

I am not writing this about my own feelings. It is the feeling of us all.

Sincerely,
Leroy E. Robinson

Hi, Darling,

Lately I have been very busy and had very little time to really sit down and write you and the children a nice long letter, due to the fact that we were short-handed. But now we have a few more cooks, so I can take a little more time with the girl that I love.

I love you, darling, and now that I am in Vietnam I love you even more.

Earlier today I went on a water run. First let me explain what a water run is. It is when we go to pick up water with trucks, for you see we have no running water here. Anyway, I had to go along as shotgun, and we had to go through their villages and believe me, honey, it is really a sight to see. As you know, I've been all over the world, but I have never seen anything like this in my life. These people are poor and suffering very bad, and the part that really hurt me was the children. They have nothing. No clothes, no food, and no place to stay.

While we waited for the truck to be filled up with water, a few of the children came up to us and begged for some food. I felt so sorry for them. I gave them all of my food. I thought about my own children, Zhayne, Shawn, and Renee. I thanked God over and over again for taking good care of them and keeping them safe.

Don't you let anyone talk about the United States, because there is no better place in the world to live in.

Now I know why I am over here. After seeing these children I would die before I let what's happening here happen there. . . .

There will be times when people will say Americans stick their nose in everyone else's business. Well, don't believe this, because this is our business. If the V.C.s take over here, it will only be a matter of years before they try the same in our own back yard. I am proud to be here doing my part, and I know that you are proud of me. God is watching over me, so we have nothing to worry about.

I love you, darling, with all my heart, and I thank God for you.

I saw a little girl the size of Renee, about four or five years old, begging for anything at all to eat. I was so hurt, I could have broken down and cried. I picked her up and gave her C-ration food. These people are also eating out of garbage cans. I could go on and on, and still I couldn't give you a full picture.

. . . . . .

> Love always,
> *Your husband*

Dear Son!

Tonight we were talking about our families at home and our children. I told my friends about you and how proud I was of you. So when I came back to my tent I decided it was time I wrote you a letter. I am going to try and tell you how I live at this base I am at, and why I am here.

Now, why am I in Vietnam? Well, it may be a little hard for you to understand completely, but Mommy will tell you more. There are people that want to take over Vietnam and take the freedom away from the Vietnamese, not let them vote or work for themselves or go from one place to another freely, like we do in the U.S. This is Communism. So we are here to help the Vietnamese people keep their freedom, and to help them keep it we have to fight, because this is the only way right now. It is just like if you had a toy and another little boy took it or tried to take it. You would first tell him it is yours and you do not want him to have it; if he still would not listen to you and tried to take it, you would then have to show him by fighting for what is yours. I have to stay in Vietnam another ten months or so, then I will be home again. By then you will be old enough to go out fishing with me. By the way, have you used that fishing rod yet? There will be lots of good times when I come home.

Well, my dear son, I think it is time I went to sleep, so give your brother and sister a kiss for me and your mother. God bless you and keep you all safe till I come home.

With all my love,
Dad

. . . . .

What is it like in Vietnam for the servicemen to hear about the protests? Well, it is very discouraging. As a matter of fact, there isn't a word to describe how we feel about the so-called U.S. citizens who are protesting about us being over here. It is bad enough that we have to be over here, let alone that we know that there are some individuals back in the U.S. who are against us.

We really don't want to be here, but there is a job to be done, and we will do it to the best of our ability. We are proud to be the ones who are fighting, instead of having some of you so-called U.S. citizens over here, because if you were here, it would just be that you people would complain constantly and the job that has to be done wouldn't get done.

The reason why we are here is to stop Communism. Most of us think that we should first get rid of the Communists back in the U.S., but the U.S. is a free country and if we didn't stop Communism over here, in due time we would no longer live in a free country. Sooner or later after the Communists took Southeast Asia, the U.S. would be one of their next objectives, and would the U.S. stop them? No, because of you protesters.

All of you think that we are here fighting only for the Vietnamese. Well, we are fighting for the Vietnamese, but we are also fighting for you.

. . . . .

My Beloved Son,

By the time this letter reaches you, it will be the anniversary of your first year of life, your first birthday. Of all the birthdays that I would like to enjoy with you, this to me seems most important. I regret that I cannot be with you, my son, for I am half-way around the world from you, in a strange land and with strange people. Nearly 12,000 miles separate me from you and your most wonderful mother; however, despite this great distance, I am with you in spirit, in my deep love and devotion for you.

I know that you are now too young to read or understand what I write and how I feel about you, but someday you shall know and understand.

Your birthday brought to your mother and me a completeness that no one else, no other one thing, could have ever provided. You have given us a joy, a happiness we had never known. In you rest all our hopes, our expectations, and our love. You have added a great purposefulness, a greater meaning to our lives.

For you, no challenge is too large to overcome, no sacrifice too great. It is for this very reason that I cannot be home with you and your mother. Instead, I am here trying to contribute what I can, in some small way, to help make this world we live in a better place for you and the many other little people like you who so much deserve the best life has to offer.

Our hopes and prayers are that you may grow up to be a fine man, keen of mind, strong of body and of character, and steeped in the spirit, the feeling of love for God, for your country and your fellow man.

These few words seem shallow in comparison to the depth of my love for you. A most happy birthday to you.

Your always devoted father,
Dad

Dear Mom,

Today the Red Cross called me and told me about my little son. It is still hard for me to believe that just two years ago Jane and I met and now we are husband and wife and the parents of a little son.

Mom, I will try to be the best son and husband and father that I possibly can. When I received the news of the baby's arrival, my heart ached for such a long time. I wanted to see him and hold him in my arms and hold his tiny hand in mine. I wanted to brush my hand across his little head and look at his sleeping face. Just to whisper in his tiny ears all the hopes and dreams I have for him would be so wonderful.

Today my thoughts slip back to the days of my childhood and to you. It is so easy now for me to understand how much of yourself you gave to us and how much you loved us.

My hopes and desires are all wrapped up in that little boy. If I can only live through this war and come home to all of you, I will raise that dear baby with the same love and devotion and patriotism that you raised us and hope to someday stand in the background and see an honest, reliable, worthwhile American and say with pride, "There goes my son." I shall ask no more of God.

> Goodnight, Mom
> Love,
> *David*

. . . . .

I guess I have never been so lonely in my life and never thought I would miss my family and friends as much as I do, and the thing bad about it is I have nine more months to go. This place makes a person really glad that he lives in the United States, and I know when I get home I will appreciate the little things more, and all the talk about the college students picketing about the draft — that sort of stuff — when I get home and someone says anything like that I'm going to knock his or her — — off 'cause those people just don't realize what we guys are going through for their freedom as well as ours.

. . . . .

> God bless you,
> Your son, *Curtis Paul*

The Face of War

"I'm in Vietnam and every day I pray for only two things—to be out of this hell and back home or to be killed before I might have to kill someone."

Dear Ma,

. . . . .

I've seen some pretty wild things so far. Something I better tell you now, and that is when I get home I'll be a nervous wreck and willing to fight anything, so you're just going to have to leave me alone until I get used to the idea of living again. I can buy six quarts of booze a month, so I decided to give up drinking for the most part. Otherwise I'll be a member of A.A. by the time I get back.

It doesn't look like I'll be home for Xmas next year. It's times like these that I wish I'd never joined, but what the hell, when I get back John and Chuck will be gone, just think of all the unhappy women I can help forget their troubles. (Read my friends this part.)

You know, I wish I had some girl to call just my own. Please ask Clancy if she will just send me a picture of Candy? To all of you I am supposed to be a man, but with Candy I can just be a scared kid, because that's all I am really, so please ask Clancy?

Well, have to go.

Love, your son,
Greg

Dear Mom and Dad,

. . . . .

Don't worry about me, I'm not about to jump off a hill or anything like that. I'm glad to be here just to make sure the States stay safe. If it takes fighting and killing to do it, then I'll fight and kill. I just can't understand why there have to be wars, or why there has to be a bunch of guys who aren't old enough to vote dying for their beliefs. I only want to do my time and go home.

. . . . .

Love,
Your son, *John*

Dearest Mother, Grandmother, and Uncle Don:

Again I sit here alone, and I wonder do I really know just how far away I am from my loved ones? At best guess, I would say that I am over ten thousand miles away from you at this very moment. That's a heck of a long way from home. Something has changed inside of me, and that is that now I feel such a closeness to you and to everyone else. Before, it was eat and run, but I always knew that I had a place to stay. I knew that there was someone there who cared about me, and I knew I had someone to turn to when I was in trouble. Here the situation is quite different. You steer for yourself and yourself only. If you are in trouble, the only reason you are sought after is because you are another rifle that they can use in this terrible war.

When I am by myself, I wonder constantly about you and all the other people who make my life so complete. Oh! I wish that I could come home tomorrow, but I can't. I just can't see why there has to be a war. Why does there always have to be armed aggression? Why don't people learn the ways of government and abide by God's laws in settling disputes? And, strange as it seems to me, in my own small way I am involved in this terrible war. To God above I pray that I return safe, to again see you and the rest of the people who mean so much to me. Mom, there are guys dying over here for our freedom — your freedom as well as mine. People not involved in this war don't know the suffering that is going on over here. You can't imagine the human suffering that these men are going through every day. Despite everything, I am proud to be a U.S. Marine and a part of this organization, although I do want to come home desperately.

How are you doing? I hope that you are all well. I read in the paper that it was 32 degrees in Kansas City. Over here, at present, it is 115 degrees, which is quite hot, and it stays hot. Some very warm southern air pushed up from Chu Lai, causing the temperature's rise. Dear Mom, take care in the year to come, and one day your son will be knocking on your door again and things will be right again. Oh, by the way, I have received the Vietnamese Service Ribbon for my actions on guard last night. We were hit by the Vietcong, and I killed three of them. I will now wear a medal for my part in this campaign.

With so much love, *Vernon*

. . . . .

How are the people taking to the war in Portland? I've read too much bullcrap about the way some of those cowardly students are acting on campuses. They sure don't show me much as far as being American citizens. They have the idea that they are our future leaders. Well, I won't follow nobody if he isn't going to help fight for my freedom.

A few weeks ago, I had the chance to talk with some Marines who had come to Okinawa for four (lousy) days of leave. They were more than happy because they had been fighting for six months with no let-up. We sat in a restaurant all the time, and I wish I could have taped it on my recorder. What they had to say would have had an impact on the people back home. One showed me where he had been shot. I asked if it hurt, and he didn't feel it. Not until after he got the — — that shot him. He was more angry than hurt. They told me of some of their patrols and how they would be talking to a buddy one minute and watch him die the next. Or wake up in the morning and see a friend hung from a tree by hooks in his armpits with parts of his body cut and shoved into his mouth. From what they said, the Vietcong aren't the only ruthless ones. *We* have to be, too. *Have* to. You'd be surprised to know that a guy you went to school with is right now shooting a nine-year-old girl and her mother. He did it because if they got the chance they would kill him. Or throwing a Vietcong out of a helicopter because he wouldn't talk.

One guy (who had broke down and cried) said that his one desire is to get enough leave to go home and kick three of those demonstrators in a well-suited place and bring him back. I tell you, it's horrible to read a paper and see your own people aren't backing you up. Now, some of those guys who beat the draft and got married are (no doubt) banging their old ladies hoping they have a baby. Spineless rats.

You will have to excuse me. I didn't mean to get so wound up on the subject, so I will stop now.

. . . . .

Dear Ruth:

When you seek someone to lay the blame upon, you can not point out one person or even one country. Most Americans blame Russia in particular, but they fail to realize that the blame also lies in the United States as well. It lies upon the students who demonstrate against our actions in Vietnam. It lies upon the president. It lies on the shoulders of every rational person in the world. In reality, we've brought it all upon ourselves.

Then you've got to think about the young soldier who gets killed in a foxhole in the middle of a jungle somewhere in Vietnam. Who does he blame?

How many potential presidents, doctors, lawyers have been brought here to fight, only to die thousands of miles from home? These men don't even have the privilege of dying on their own soil. Yet they still come, willingly, to do their part for a country they never heard of until a very few years ago.

But this is wrong also. They are actually fighting for the entire world in the hope that someday the whole world will be free.

Maybe this is the real reason. But we can't help asking ourselves why. Why are we fighting in the first place? Do you know? Does anybody know? I don't.

I suppose it all stems back to the Bible. If everyone believed in the Bible and practiced what it preaches, then we wouldn't be fighting. It's all laid out before us; why don't we accept it?

. . . . .

Love,

Don

. . . . .

I'm in Vietnam and every day I pray for only two things —
to be out of this hell and back home or to be killed before I might
have to kill someone.

The going here is pretty rough, and all the dirty fighting isn't
on one side. A week ago our platoon leader brought in three
prisoners. I was part of the group that brought them in. They set
up a questioning station, and someone from Intelligence was doing
the questioning. This was the first time I saw anything like this
and found out that we use dirty methods, too.

This guy from Intelligence had all three lined up. One was a
woman. He stripped her down to the waist and stripped the two
men all the way. He had a little gadget I thought was a walkie-
talkie or something. He stuck one end of this wire to the lady's
chest and it was a kind of electric shock, because she got a real
bad burn. From what she was screaming, my buddy and I could
figure she didn't know anything.

Then they took this same wire and tried it on the lady's husband
and brother, but on their lower parts. I grabbed the damn thing
and stuck it to the backass of the guy from Intelligence.

Ever since that day I've been sick to my stomach and haven't
been out on patrol or anything. My sergeant tells me I'm suffering from battle fatigue and might get sent home.

We wish we could send you a couple of those electrical gadgets
to use on the powers that sent and keep us here. This must end
soon or a lot of us will go nuts.

. . . . .

My lovely Lynn,

I wanted to write you a letter that would fit this Thanksgiving
Day, so I sat down last night, but found myself lost for words.

It was about six-thirty in the evening and rather hot, so I thought
I'd take a walk before writing. I walked down toward the motor
pool. As I neared Graves Registration a copter came swooping
down with a gust of wind. I stood there watching as the wind died
down, and from the copter a red flashing light seemed to be the
only movement about.

Then I saw at first two men, then four, all bearing litters. They
carried the litters to the copter. Then the men returned to the tent